What communication professionals are saying about
"30 Things You Should Know About Media Relations"

"Dealing with media coverage can be seen as a minefield for the uninitiated, but former television reporter Tim Herrera does a tremendous job of demystifying how the news business works. That insight, delivered in a breezy anecdotal style, will be a valuable and credible tool for anyone seeking an understanding of how to deal with reporters and press coverage...and remain standing."

-Kevin Riggs, Sr. Vice President
Randle Communications, Sacramento

"30 Things You Should Know About Media Relations" is a concise and eminently useful handbook. Tim Herrera has produced a valuable tool for anyone who works with media, from novice to grizzled pro. Don't be misled by the title, Herrera provides *hundreds* of tips on how to better communicate with the media.

-Steve O'Donoghue, Director
California Scholastic Journalism Initiative

"A step-by-step guide with wonderfully blunt advice for the small/medium sized organization faced with developing a communications plan. No director of a small or medium sized organization should consider themselves media savvy until they've read this book."

-Dana Howard, Sunday Open House - Real Estate Media

"Tim's unique experiences on both sides of the media fence make this THE book on effective media relations for small businesses and organizations. Reading it will give you with the tools you need to be successful in your publicity efforts."

-Maddie Blunck, Corporate Communications Director
Marquis Spas

"This book offers affordable suggestions for non-profits and small businesses looking to get the attention of the media on a variety of different platforms. Thank you, Tim Herrera, for sharing your professional insight and experience on this topic."

-Angela Quisumbing, M.A.
Founder & Editor
The Pinky Project/Mira Mesa Mom

"Knowing how to do something is never as important as knowing *why* to do it. Fortunately, Tim knows both and he's written a bootstrapper's bible of media relations. "Do it yourself" doesn't mean "do it alone" any more."

-Joel D Canfield, Someday Box, Author
Coaching and Independent Publishing

30 Things You Should Know About Media Relations

Second Edition

A Communications Survival Guide for Small Businesses, Nonprofits and Community Groups

"The greatest problem in communication is the illusion that it has been accomplished."

- George Bernard Shaw

Table of Contents

What you'll learn from this book!

about You

INTRODUCTION

Welcome to the second edition of *30 Things You Should Know about Media Relations*. While working on the update, I was thinking of using something snappy in the title like "2.0", or "Now contains more fiber" but I think that was too much. People are immune to those terms now anyway. So, while this is an upgrade from the previous edition, it probably has the same amount of fiber. This book still contains valuable information on how to connect with the media and what to do once you connect, but it also contains new material on strategic communication planning and social networking. These are very important THINGS in this updated version of 30 THINGS.

One of your primary goals – and the reason you bought this book – is that you want to have your group or organization featured on the local evening news or in the local paper. You are an attention seeker, but in the right way. Getting local coverage will increase your group's exposure. Having a regional online publication profile your nonprofit organization could bring in more volunteers or donations. If you are a business operator, it will hopefully mean more clients and customers. If you are a small community group, one spot on the evening news might inform an entire media market about your cause or concerns. This book will help you figure out how to make the right connections in a manageable fashion. This book will also show you how to connect with stakeholders without the media!

When I worked as a reporter, one thing that I noticed when covering stories involving small businesses, nonprofit organizations and local community groups is that most of them are in serious need of media relations guidance, but they can't afford it. Hiring professional help in this area is expensive, often worth it, but expensive just the same. These groups have great stories to tell but they are not sure how to make those connections.

Some companies and organizations have enough room in their budgets to hire media relations and public relations professionals, but the smaller ones have to do without, or they do it themselves and struggle through. If you <u>can</u> afford professional media relations help, then hire someone! But if you <u>can't</u> afford to hire professional help, then this is the book for you.

As you work your way through this book, I hope you'll notice that I've tried to keep things simple and make everything easy to follow. Hopefully this is exactly what you need to start making media connections and to start letting people know more about your small business, nonprofit organization or local community group.

This book, containing 30 simple tips for better media relations covers the basics and is not designed to serve as an all-purpose marketing/public relations/communications guide. The sole purpose of this book is to provide you with basic information that will help you get started in reaching out to the media.

Thanks and good luck!

Tim Herrera
Author

Before We Start

"Know thyself, know thy enemies. In a thousand battles,
win a thousand victories."
- Confucius

If you own a major corporation or run a nationally known organization, then this book is not for you. That is, unless you like helping out struggling authors. Why is this book NOT for the big guys? Because they already have either a large communications department at their disposal or have enough money to hire a high-powered public relations firm to help them work with the media. However, if you own a small, local company or run a local, community-based organization, then this is the book for you. It's likely that you don't have a communications person, let alone a media relations department. And there's no way that you can afford to pay a public relations firm to help with media relations. If that's the case... keep reading and make use of each of the 30 things.

There's a mystery surrounding the media. Many people who don't work in it don't really know how the media operates. Those folks who rarely, if ever, come in contact with a reporter or journalist don't understand the process. How do reporters select the stories they cover? How do news organizations decide whom to use for sources in stories? If a business or community group is involved in a negative news story, is there any possible way that a positive can come out of that negative?

The average person will never need to know the inner workings of a newsroom, and that's okay. The average person who does not have regular contact with the media – and has no plans on making contact – has no need to know how a news operation actually operates. However, if you are a business owner, an executive with a nonprofit organization or the operator of a community based organization and you don't have a working knowledge of the news business... that's not okay. You are cheating yourself out of golden opportunities. If you do not know how to use today's tools like the Internet, Facebook, Twitter and YouTube, that's not okay either.

As I mentioned above, Confucius did once say, "Know thy enemies" but that does not mean you need to consider the media your enemy! It means that you should know how that business operates. And if you know how the media operate then you know what the media needs to get the job done. That's what this book is all about; it's about unraveling the mystery surrounding the media – newspaper, television and radio.

Many of us have heard the complaint about the alleged "MEDIA CONSPIRACY." I am here to tell you that after more than two decades as a television news reporter, radio news reporter and news director, newspaper columnist, free-lance writer, author, public information officer, media consultant, and college instructor that the conspiracy is a great myth. The notion of a conspiracy suggests there is a great deal of organization, and the news business overall is not organized enough to plan a conspiracy. If all the great media moguls ever decided to get together and form a conspiracy then the result would be like herding cats into a swimming pool. It just wouldn't happen!

My entire reporting career was spent on the local level in Dallas, Pittsburgh and Sacramento. I was never a network correspondent or a reporter for a nationally known newspaper. I *have* been a local market news foot soldier dealing on an everyday basis with people who have tried unsuccessfully to avoid being in the news and folks who have tried, equally unsuccessfully, to get some local press. I've had countless TV stories run on CNN, NBC and affiliates throughout the country but it is news on the local level that I really understand and can help you with. And getting local news coverage is what you want to learn how to accomplish. It is where you want to start. You need the knowledge to do that. This book offers you that.

Knowledge is the key to success in dealing with the press. In all of my years as a reporter and writer, I cannot tell you how many times I crossed paths with a business owner, community group organizer and even a public official who did not know how to work with the media, and it showed. So many merchants and activists miss out on countless opportunities to get their messages across because they are not clear on who to contact, how to contact them and, most importantly, what to say when making contact.

This book, short, to the point and filled with 30 helpful tips, will strip away all the varnish and get you right down to the natural wood of the news business.

Here is why this book will be helpful to you: It will help you remember that the only thing worse than a business owner, nonprofit chief or community activist who doesn't know how the media operates is one who truly believes he or she understands the process but is dead wrong. That can do more harm than good because it can soil relationships before they have a chance to flourish. Like the old saying goes, "a little bit of knowledge is a dangerous thing."

This book will help you attain the goal of working with the media and the media working with you. It is possible to form a partnership of sorts. Your goal is never to "get that reporter in your back pocket" because those efforts backfire. Reporters and editors know when someone is trying to "use them." Your goal is to reach a level of "media consciousness" that will help you get your message out and get your name or your firm's name out there too.

The most important thing to remember is to not fear the media. Sometimes it stings, but its bark is worse than its bite. Remember, the media is not something to avoid – like cleaning out the garage or washing to dog. If you can attain a better level of awareness of how the media works then you are well on your way to helping your organization and yourself succeed.

If your goal is to gain national notoriety and launch a nationwide media blitz, you might be better suited to hire a well-oiled and well-connected public relations firm. Hopefully, you'll have the money to do that. If you can shoot some kind of video that goes viral on YouTube and you are thrust into the national spotlight, then good for you. But if you are just trying to learn more about the local news business, learn how to make the right contacts with your local reporters and get your message out there, then this book will help you.

In advance, I say "you're welcome."

What you'll learn from this book...

Consider this book a condensed version of a long and involved media relations how-to guide, minus tons of data, case studies and research that you don't really have time to read right now. This is a press relations starter kit. This book is purposely brief to make it easier to follow. By the time you are finished with this book you will:

- Have a better idea of what the media is looking for when producing news stories

- Understand the complex role of the communications professional

- Know how to construct a media relations and communications plan

- Understand the importance of determining your target audience and how to reach out to people

- Become familiar with the many different ways to reach out to whoever it is that makes up your target audience

- How to write media advisories, press releases and organize press conferences

- Learn how to conduct yourself during interviews and press conferences

- Learn the dos and don'ts of media relations

- Understand how to gauge your success in making media connections

- Understand that the simple tools to accomplish your goals are within your reach.

Thing 1

Help Journalists Do Their Jobs and They Will Help YOU Do YOURS

Learn How to Work with the Media...

Just like all characters portrayed in movies, the reporter is often stereotyped to make that person more interesting and larger than life. The reporter on the big screen is relentless. He or she will do just about anything to get the story. He or she will work hour after hour neglecting personal lives – and often even personal hygiene - in pursuit of the big story. The reporter will forgo food, sleep and miss important events like children's birthday parties just to snag that one colossal story. In summary, let me say that – for the most part – that's _not_ accurate!

Reporters are generally regular people with interesting jobs who are trying to manage their careers around their regular lives. As far as the movie version of the reporter goes, their depictions by Hollywood have typically been less than accurate. Their images are pumped up and exaggerated. And why not? People want excitement. They do not want to see movies about the mundane aspects of any profession. For example, people would not pay to see films about police officers filling out paperwork or waiting for hours on end in courthouse hallways waiting to testify at trials.

Defense lawyer: "Officer, where were you on the night of August 13th?"

Officer: "Well, I was sitting in my squad car, all alone in the parking lot of the International House of Pancakes filling out a burglary report. You see, the form has seventy-five slots that need to be filled and after I put in the day and date and the list of missing articles... and just as I was filling out space number-52 when I spilled my latte and...."

Defense lawyer: "Um... no further questions, your honor. The jury is asleep."

Not many folks would fork over $10 a ticket to watch an auto racing film in which the main characters only work on engines.

"Dewey, I said give me the three-quarter wrench, not the half-inch! Stat! We're losing her!"

The camera zooms in on Dewey's face as he struggles with the deep internal conflict over not being able to tell the difference between the three-quarter and the half-inch.

Reporters, editors and interviewers are regular people who work and then go home at the end of the day. The journalism field is filled with a great many ambitious people who don't stop digging until they find the true dirt – the Holy Grail – and who want nothing better than to uncover that nugget of information that leads to a Congressional hearing and eventually the impeachment of a President or the discrediting of a Televangelist. However, most journalists are regular people with regular lives who are just trying to find interesting stories to report. (Perhaps your story is interesting!)

Many movies and television shows often portray journalists as tireless pursuers of the truth who will not stop until they get the information they are seeking and see it in print or on the tube. That's a mild overstatement of reality. For the most part, reporters are people who are trying to file their stories in time to make it to their child's school play or soccer game. Most reporters are just doing a job they enjoy, while earning a good living that enables them to get home in time to kiss their kids good night and spend time with their spouse.

For the most part, members of the media are regular folks who are just looking for good stories to tell. What's important to remember is that maybe you are the type of person who has a good story to tell – about your group, your company, and your program – but you don't know how to get that done.

You can get that done in one of three ways, by being:

- **Cooperative**
- **Courteous**
- **Calm**

You will find these concepts throughout this book, sometimes in an obvious manner, but most of the times subliminally. All three of these concepts work hand-in-hand. By following these simple ideas, you will get a leg up on others in your quest for a better understanding of how the media works and how you can work with the media.

First, let's talk about being **cooperative**. When considering this step, it is important to follow the wise advice of the immortal Mark Twain who once said: "Never pick fights with people who buy their ink by the barrel!"

When you do make contact with a reporter, or vice versa, understand the rules of engagement and how to get around problems that you see arising.

Understand that cooperation is possible. While reporters have often-immovable deadlines, unbelievable time constraints and ask intrusive questions, it is possible to work within their parameters in a cooperative way to achieve mutual goals.

Let's say that you get a call from a reporter for one of your local newspapers – pretending for a moment that you live in one of those cities fortunate to have more than one local newspaper – and that reporter is seeking some information.

"I am doing a story on the great decline of the widget industry and since you are a foremost authority on widgets it was suggested that I call you," the reporter says. "I am in a bind because my regular widget source is unavailable because of his indictment on corporate fraud. My deadline is in one hour. Can you help me?"

If you are faced with a situation like this and can cooperate in some way, then you have scored major points with this frantic reporter.

"I can offer you some overall comments on the widget empire I have built and I can explain the creation of a widget, from concept to construction, and I can explain why I believe the industry as a whole is struggling. But if you ask me to comment on competitors facing fraud charges, I can't go there," you answer.

"Sounds great!" the relieved reporter says – and you are on your way.

Reporters often need interviews and information right away and are on tight schedules. Explain to them that you also have a tight schedule and want to accommodate their needs by carving out time for an interview. If it means rescheduling an appointment or skipping lunch that day, **do it.** Explain to the calling journalist that you are doing some "schedule shuffling" and he or she will appreciate your efforts.

Through cooperation you are beginning to establish a press contact. However, please remember that cooperation is and should be a two-way street and that's something the reporter should realize. You do not have to be a pushover but you can assist this reporter in getting his or her job done.

Once you have reached an understanding of cooperation, also understand that being **courteous** is necessary to get the job done.

While the majority of journalists are bright and thoughtful people, there are many working in the trade who are pushy and impatient. They are under a great deal of pressure to gather information and to do so at lightning speed. They want the information yesterday if not sooner and they will push extremely hard sometimes to get it. If the reporter calling you is courteous, then as a member of polite society you should be courteous in return. However, if the caller is rude and discourteous it would be in your best interest to at least feign your "courteousness" during this encounter.

Let's say the scribe seeking widget information calls you and demands: "I am uncovering the greatest corporate widget scandal of all time. I only have an hour until my deadline. I am going to ask you some questions and you will answer them!"

Do you have an obligation to answer? No. This caller is obviously a jerk and thinks that just because he won a few journalist awards and once shook hands with Wolf Blitzer at a Dairy Queen (*I wonder if Wolf likes Oreo blizzards!*) that he can treat you like dirt. The best way to handle this is to remain courteous because – well, that's the way your mother raised you.

"I'm sorry," you say. "I really can't address those issues at this time, especially on such short notice. Perhaps with more notice, I would be glad to help you the next time you want to talk about the wonderful world of widgets."

In this hypothetical instance, even though the reporter was mean and pushy, you were kind and courteous. Now, please note that most reporters would not be as unpleasant as the one we created. The majority of journalists in the business today are honest, hard-working people. Most of them understand that if they treat interview subjects poorly that they risk getting crummy cooperation in return.

What is important to remember is that by being courteous and helpful that you are laying the groundwork for establishing a good relationship with this reporter and his publication or broadcast operation. The next time that reporter needs a source in the widget industry – either for a positive or negative story – that reporter will think of you first because you were courteous.

So, we have seen how **cooperation** and **courtesy** work together in dealing with a reporter. The third point to consider now is the art of being **calm.**

There's an old saying in the news business that you know you are going to have a bad day when you go to work and find a 60 Minutes crew waiting to speak to you. If something like this ever happens to you – it could, but it would be rare – the thing to remember is to remain calm. It never pays to panic.

If at all possible, be Zen-like.

Hang loose, dude.

Use the force, Luke!

Too many television news programs and magazine shows are littered with excerpts of potential interview subjects acting jumpy and scared and saying what is probably the worst thing any interview subject can say – **NO COMMENT**. (We will confront the dreaded "No Comment" issue later.)

Panicky interview subjects act the way they do for two reasons: the reporter frightened the snot out of them and, they did not remain calm. Remaining calm is easier said than done, but it is achievable once you have the right tools.

This book will provide you with those tools.

The odds of you being chased down by a news reporter firing off pointed questions that make you want to run and hide are slim to none. The chances are greater that a reporter will call you and request some information about your organization and your industry, or an issue with which your group is associated. If and when this does happen, it is important to stay calm and consider this phone call from the press an **opportunity** to tell the world something about what you do. Consider it a chance to get some publicity.

Here are some helpful **Things** to consider when trying remaining calm before, during or after an interview:

- Take a deep breath during each question to soothe your nerves.
- Think carefully before answering, so long as you don't drag out your response with prolonged silence and a blank stare.
- It's okay to say "I don't have an answer for that now but will get back to you."
- Keep in mind the "key messages" you want to make and place them within your responses. (We'll talk about key messages later on.)
- Ask the reporter to "repeat the question" if you are not sure what point he or she is trying to make.
- Think of the interview as a "conversation" with someone wanting to know more about you and what you do.

Also keep in mind that all of this gets easier with practice. Rome wasn't built in a day and someone like Steve Jobs of Apple Computer fame probably wasn't a dynamic interview subject right out of the gate. The more interviews you do, the easier it gets. And by remembering and applying the key concepts of **cooperation, courtesy** and **calm** you will find yourself confidently handling every interview opportunity.

Thing 2

DON'T Avoid the Media

Remember That Media Can Equal Opportunity

There probably have been plenty of times when you have had to turn away a salesman at your door by saying something like this; "Look, I really don't need your combination floor wax/poultry marinade product but thanks for coming by my home at dinner time!"

Well, maybe in that case opportunity was NOT knocking. However, in many cases it can come knocking when it comes to a call out of the blue from a local media outlet to you. (The rhyming was accidental and won't happen again.) An unexpected call from a reporter to your organization or place of business is something that you can use to generate some publicity for yourself or your operation.

I can recall one specific instance of seeing "opportunity knock" for a small company when I was working as a television news reporter in Sacramento. The names of these companies have been changed to protect the innocent. Actually, everyone is innocent here but I still won't use the actual names of those involved.

The assignment was a news story on Internet security, what concerns companies might have and what business owners could do to protect themselves. This came on the heels of a number of nasty virus outbreaks crippling company e-mail systems throughout the world. It was a hot news topic at the time.

As a reporter I always found that if I needed interviews from people in the business sector that it worked best to contact small, locally owned companies when requesting interviews. Dealing with big chain company stores was always a hassle because of the layers of bureaucracy you had to go through to get permission to get inside a store to take pictures and get interviews. Medium sized to smaller companies always worked best for me because I could talk to the owner – or someone within earshot of the owner – to get the necessary ingredients for a good story.

In this case I am describing, let's say there were two small companies from which to choose, both of them top-notch when it comes to web page design and web security, both of them are well known in the local cyber-community as well run companies. We'll call these companies "CYBER GUYS" and "GEEKS-R-US."

The phone call to the first company went like this:

REPORTER: I am doing this story about web security and what companies can do to guard against cyber-attacks. Can we come over, shoot some video of your company and interview you about what safeguards people can take?

CYBERGUYS: Are you doing this because of the latest viruses?

REPORTER: Yes, it's impacting a lot of companies.

CYBERGUYS: Well, we don't want our customers to think that we have questionable security. We don't want to be a part of that story.

REPORTER: Maybe I didn't explain myself well enough. The story is not about you or your customers being victims, or being hurt by what your company has or has not done. It's about you giving people advice about what they can do to protect their home and business computers. It's a chance to talk about your business.

CYBERGUYS: "I don't think so. You are going to use the word "virus" and "Cyberguys" in the same story. I don't think that's good for us. People will think our security stinks."

I could not make the Cyberguys person understand that I was not trying to paint his business in a bad light. I was hoping to use his company to help explain to **thousands and thousands** of viewers the problems caused by these virus outbreaks and what can be done to prevent them. Unfortunately, the guy never got the point and I never called that company for a news story again.

That is a true and accurate depiction of the conversation... with a little paraphrasing thrown in. Even though I explained to the business owner that I was not focusing on his company as having a problem, but that I was focusing on his firm to help viewers (who are also potential customers) prevent computer virus attacks, my message did not get through. All Mr. Cyberguy heard was the word "virus" and thought the story would reflect negatively on him. He could not see that it was actually an **opportunity** to get his company name out there and to talk about what solutions they offer customers, but he didn't answer when opportunity knocked.

Let's step aside for a moment and reflect on one aspect that's very important here. When a reporter calls requesting information and tells you what his or her story is about, you have to believe that person is telling you the truth. You have to trust he or she is telling you and take it at face value. Before you agree to allow a reporter to question you, you have the right to question the reporter to determine exactly what is expected from you during an interview. If a reporter tells you one thing over the phone and then takes another approach once you make contact, then you have the right to terminate the interview and contact that reporter's boss and complain.

So, CYBERGUYS didn't want to be part of a story that addresses the computer virus problem in which they could offer helpful advice and solutions even after I pointed out it was a chance for them to get their name out there and tell the local, money spending public what they do. Rather than giving up and risking the possibility of having a news manager bark at me like an angry drill sergeant, I pressed on and contacted GEEKS-R-US. The folks there had a completely different approach to this opportunity. Again, I am paraphrasing.

GEEKS-R-US: We do web page design and security, and you want to take pictures of our company and let us tell people how to address potential computer problems?

REPORTER: Yes.

GEEKS-R-US: And who else will be featured in the story?

REPORTER: I am using a network feed interview with Bill Gates from Microsoft and…

GEEKS-R-US: Wait a minute. You'll let me talk about what our business does to help people protect themselves and Bill Gates will be in the story too?

REPORTER: Yes.

GEEKS-R-US: I am free in a half-hour. See you then.

Let's review.

Where CYBERGUYS saw risk, GEEKS-R-US saw potential. Maybe Mr. CYBERGUY was having a rough day and was dealing with a computer virus himself. Or maybe he didn't see the potential for getting the equivalent of free advertising. On the other hand, the people at GEEKS-R-US opened up their doors and allowed their company to be used as a prop for telling a news story. It was a chance for the owner's face to be on television and superimposed beneath his face were his name and GEEKS-R-US in large letters. This appearance on a television news program may not have changed his company's bottom line for the final quarter of that fiscal year, but it did provide his growing company with the opportunity to have its name spoken and flashed before thousands if not hundreds of thousands of potential customers.

One thing for you to remember – whether you run a small company, a nonprofit organization or a community based organization – is that in many cases there is a simple equation that comes into play, and that is that your company plus media interviews can equal free positive publicity.

Here is a list of a few things to keep in mind regarding the media:

- Remind yourselves that media coverage can be an opportunity to "sell" your programs and accomplishments.

- Remember; don't ignore the media because you will miss opportunities to promote your programs, your people and your achievements.

- Media educates the public and influences public opinion. In doing your planning, think of how you can use media coverage to your advantage to educate people about your group or organization and how you can help influence public opinion.

- Be a source and a resource. When reporters contact you, you need to be able to provide good quotes as well as solid background information.

- Be willing and able to send reporters to other places and other people where they can get information. Especially the information that you WANT them to get.

- Remember: press coverage and media attention can be just as effective if not more effective as any other type of advertising.

It is probably hard for many people to believe that there is actually opportunity involved in a situation in which media scrutiny is concerned. But it is true and it is possible. Although it might not happen with every occasion, contact with the media can and often does equal opportunity.

On the flip side, don't assume that every time a reporter calls or every time that you come in contact with a journalist that it means you are guaranteed an opportunity to get on television or be quoted in the newspaper singing the praises of your group or business. Life doesn't work that way. Neither does the media. More than likely, a reporter has called you for two reasons: he or she is working on a story that would be of interest to or involving your group, company or industry, or your own outfit is into something pretty deep.

If your group is into some kind of media mess, then you are in need of some serious crisis management help. Media crisis management is an art form in itself. (We'll touch on that a little later in this book.) Proper planning will help you deal with those crisis situations. If you have a plan in place, your chances of both avoiding and properly dealing with a media crisis are fairly good.

You might be asking yourself this question: why not ignore the media? The news is all about fires, floods, kidnappings, natural disasters, wars and Hollywood stars going to rehab, right? Don't more people get their information from Google anyway? If I ignore the press it will go away and leave me alone, right? I don't want to be a part of that, do I? The answer is: well, maybe you DO want to be part of it if it can be helpful to you in some way.

I am not advocating that you – as a business owner or representative of a community based organization – find a way to interject yourselves into the news of the day, or some ongoing big news story, as a way of "getting your name out there." But take a look at what's going on in the news to see if there's a way that you or your organization can become involved in order to get some name recognition while helping reporters with their stories.

Let's use our example about operating a business in an area that needs more positive attention and maybe even some POSITIVE MEDIA COVERAGE. So, one day you look out your company's front window and see a television news photographer outside shooting some video. You have a couple of choices here: you can go out and ask the guy what he's doing and why, or you can ignore him and hope he doesn't take pictures of your shop.

Suppose you go outside and strike up a conversation:

YOU: Hi, what are you doing out here?

PHOTOGRAPHER: We're doing a story on businesses trying to make it in a tough economy?

YOU: Well, I'm a business owner trying to make it in a tough economy.

PHOTOGRAPHER: Well, can we interview you?

YOU: Sure!

Yeah, I know. That was a simplistic and rare example. But it could be an opportunity for you to become part of a news story that could place your name and the name of your business in the local news. If you get your name on the local news station then someone will see it and it is possible that event could create business for you. Anything is possible!

Perhaps that news crew is doing a story on traffic, or an increase in crime, or the need for road improvements. Whatever the situation, being interviewed by a local news crew can help you start to build a relationship with the media. So, the next time that crew is doing a story on a topic or issue that involves your line of work then there's a good chance that crew will want to speak with you again.

Thing 3

Understand What News Stories ARE and ARE NOT

What interests the media? It's not an easy question to answer.

A.J. Liebling, an American journalist who did a lot of writing for the *New Yorker* during his reporting days once said: "People everywhere confuse what they read in the newspapers with news."

That brings us to the age-old question: what makes a news story interesting enough to attract the media? There's really no definitive answer to that question because sometimes it just depends on the day. Some news days are busier than others and your event, the one you have been planning for months, just does not interest the press the day that your event is being held. There's nothing you can do about that. You can lead reporters to your story but if they don't find it interesting you can't make them actually report on it.

Here are some general reasons that a news organization might find something you are doing worth covering:

- Your story has real or potential community impact
- There's relevance to an ongoing issue or community need
- There's a connection, or "tie-in" with an ongoing story or larger interest or a "tie-in", with a national holiday or observance
- Is your story visual? (Both for television and newspapers. Remember, newspapers need great photos!)
- If your story is unique in some way
- Convenience—if the time, place and location of your

story easily fits into the plans of the media outlet
- Credibility—both your credibility and the credibility of those who are connected with you, your organization or your event
- Celebrity involvement
- If there is large community participation

To be honest, news often is hard to define. Editors will tell you that news has to be interesting, entertaining, shocking, intriguing or funny. It can be something that affects a lot of people, or sometimes maybe just a small segment of the population, or even just one person. By definition, news is something that's new. However, old topics get coverage too. Like I said, news often is hard to define.

Please keep in mind that your story or event could have most of these attributes and still not attract media interest. Many times news coverage depends on several factors: staffing availability at the news operations on the day or your event, or if there's big, breaking news story somewhere else. News crews get diverted all of the time. It just happens.

The bottom line is that there is no tried and true hook that will guarantee media coverage for you. Many times the negative aspects of a story gets coverage, and with good reason. For example: read the following two samples and decide for yourselves which one is more worthy of media coverage, at least in the eyes of a news manager.

Example "A": There's a local electronics store in your community that has on its shelves several old model computers. They still are in fine working condition, but because they don't have all the bells and whistles compared to the latest models, they are considered obsolete. Mr. Electronics Store owner decides that he'd like to take the remaining computers – let's say there are dozens of them – and donate them to the local community center. At the local center, people can use the computers to work on reports, resumes, do homework, or whatever they need. The mayor, local city council, and some school board members decide to hold a special ceremony and thank Mr. Electronics Store owner for his generosity. They are even naming the new computer room after him.

Example "B": There's a break-in at a local community center. The burglars vandalized the place, and stole the new computers donated by Mr. Electronics Store owner. The mayor, local city council and school board members are angry. Children who used the computer equipment to do their homework are victimized.

So, which example is **more likely** to generate news coverage? The answer is "B". Unfortunately, stories involving crime and victimization tend to be covered more often than stories about people doing nice things and communities coming together. It's just one of the "news facts of life." However, that should not discourage you from trying to garner positive news coverage.

There are reporters in newsrooms all across the country searching for positive news stories to cover. Sometimes they just can't get the approval to report those stories from the people above them on the media outlet food chain. But keep trying. Positive, solution oriented stories do creep their way into local news coverage now and again. Maybe your positive story will be the next one.

Media interest checklist

Now take time to answer that question...

Put together a list of ten reasons why you believe your group, organization or business would be of interest to the media. Why should the public be interested in "your story"?

1)

2)

3)

4)

5)

6)

7)

8)

9)

10)

Thing 4

The Importance of Strategic Communications Planning

Developing a Strategic Communications Plan

Ask yourself some questions...

- What is the issue?
- What is the solution?
- Who can help you create change?
- Who needs to be mobilized?

The great philosopher and Hall of fame baseball player Yogi Berra once said, "If you don't know where you are going, you are certain to end up somewhere else." That is true in life, and in communications. If you are planning to launch a fundraising campaign, a volunteer recruiting drive, or if you want to increase your customer base – and you are planning on implementing a communications component to get the word out– you really need to develop a strategic communications plan.

Some companies, groups and governmental bodies like to have a procedural plan written out for media. It's good to have guidelines.

This is an opportunity to map out in detail exactly what you're involved with or facing. When formulating your communications plan it's good to ask yourself **"What's the issue?"** What we mean by "issue" is the topic of concern. What's got you all in a ruffle, or what are you hoping to get others all in a ruffle about? Sometimes seeing these things written down will help you make more sense of things.

Then you need to pose this question: **What's the solution?** This is usually the solution you'd most like to see. It's kind of like visualization, seeing the answer right before you. It's kind of like when we searched the back of the algebra book for answers to problems we struggled with while in school. We had the question, and then we read the answer in the back of the book. Then we figured out what to do to get to the right answer. In this case involving media management, have the answer to your problem figured out and work toward it. Think of it as reverse engineering.

Another question: **Who can help you create change?** In answering this question, you will actually come up with more than one list. First, you should put together a list of people you are trying to reach with your message. These people could be new customers, new members, or local politicians. The list can be limitless. Also put together a list of people that you feel might "represent well". These are people who could speak on your behalf or serve as solid references. (We'll get to the topic of selecting spokespeople later on in this book.)

Finding people who could "represent well" will come in extremely handy if you are putting together a task force or some kind of ad hoc committee. Finally, if you do not already have an established list of media contacts that can help circulate your message, then this is the time to start developing one.

Who needs to be mobilized? When putting together a media plan, think about which people or community leaders to recruit. Again, if you are assembling a task force or community group this is a useful list to have for many reasons.

It is also important that you develop a **central theme** for your project, like a mission statement but not as formal. Write one sentence stating "what this is all about" and follow that sentence.

For instance, let's say your goal is to recruit new members for your social organization. Make that your statement: "We want to recruit more members, increase our numbers and become more influential." Once you start building on a statement like that then your chances of success will increase.

Finally, identify the **"power holders"** in your community: community leaders, parents, students, teachers, legislators, state officials, business owners. These are the folks who are right in the center of your target's bulls-eye. Keep them in mind as you are directing your message toward them.

So, what is strategic communications planning? It means what the name implies. Not only do you need to develop a plan, but you have to be strategic about it. Each aspect that you design has to have meaning. There has to be a reason behind each move that you make when developing your blueprint.

So, what is strategic communications planning? It means you as the leader of a small business, nonprofit organization or community group must use communications to create or strengthen connections with your key audiences. It's the development of a master plan. If you were planning a cross country road trip from San Francisco to Atlanta, would you travel without a trusty map, or a functional GPS system? I would not recommend it.

When developing a strategic communications plan, you are creating a flexible framework to identify your goals, audiences, methods of transmitting your message, and methods of evaluation. Benjamin Franklin, founding father and currency face model, once said "By failing to prepare, you are preparing to fail." By developing your strategic communications plan, you are improving the chances that you will not fail in getting your message out there.

Now, in the previous paragraph you might have noticed that I called this a "flexible framework." What do I mean by that? Show of hands, please! By that I mean that few plans are perfect and go off without any complications. While developing your plan, you must be willing to make changes along the way if you notice that your initial strategy is not working.

You can lay out all of your challenges in front of you to see what roadblocks to steer around. Here is a listing of elements contained in a very basic strategic communications plan.

- Executive Summary
- Background
- Situation Analysis/SWOT
- Core Problem/Opportunity
- Goals and Objectives
- Key Publics and Messages
    - Message strategy to each
    - Recommended strategies
    - Recommended strategies for making presentation to media representatives
- Calendar
- Budget
- Evaluation – Course Re-direction?

Let's go into more detail about each one of these areas. This should give you a better idea of why each of these areas is important and why they rely on each other for support.

Executive Summary: In a clear and concise way, using 200 words or less, write an overview of your project. You want to sum up the key points of your plan for your readers who, in this case, would be people connected to your organization who might need to know about, or approve this plan. If anything, this executive summary would help keep you on track so that you don't lose focus. Executive summaries save readers time and help prepare them for the upcoming content and are sometimes called the most important part of any plan.

Background: This is a brief summary of the entire situation and why you need to develop this plan. Again, in 200 words or less, describe the situation, and the players involved. A brief organizational history is good, but don't go as far back as the dawn of time.

Situation Analysis/SWOT: This is where you write a brief analysis of your situation. **SWOT** stands for Strengths, Weaknesses, Opportunities and Threats. This is a useful tool for any organization that wants to develop a deeper understanding of what to do in any decision-making situation. It is always a good idea to do your SWOT Analysis during a brainstorming session, so that you can get flooded with good examples. However, it is best to whittle your list down to a manageable number. The primary purpose of this analysis is to assemble a list of relevant aspects, and then search for answers to them. You can always do these in the form of a chart, like this:

Strengths	Weaknesses
1.	1.
2.	2.
3.	3.
4.	4.
5.	5.
Opportunities	Threats
1.	1.
2.	2.
3.	3.
4.	4.
5.	5.

Core Problem/Opportunity: I guess to be very direct; I would say that in this age of political correctness and overuse of cheery and positive words, that both "core problem" and "opportunity" are really the same thing. Some folks insist on using the word opportunity instead of problem because they believe it is a more positive approach. To that I say, whatever makes you happy. However, whichever word you decide to use, take some time to sit down and really figure out your core problem/opportunity is. It is your main reason for developing this strategic communications plan. Don't just write a sentence or two. Really explore all angles of the problem/opportunity that you are facing. Explore all of the angles.

Goals and Objectives: These are not interchangeable words. Goals and objectives are different. Your goals are your general intentions. They are broad in nature. They are almost like intangibles. Objectives are narrow and more precise. While goals really cannot be validated or quantified, objectives can be validated and quantified. For example, let's say one of the main reasons you are developing a strategic communications plan is that you want to increase membership in your nonprofit organization. So, let's say that your GOAL would be "increase membership". Can that really be validated? Well, sort of. But can it be quantified? Not really. Now, let's say that your OBJECTIVE is to "increase group membership by 10-percent" by July of this year. Can you quantify that? Absolutely!

Why create lists of goals and objectives? It is good practice to create targets, both broad and specific. Every organization or group needs benchmarks to reach for and try to attain. You need to have goals and objectives.

Key Publics and Messages: This is where you make a list of the important people you are trying to reach with this strategic communications plan. I would recommend that you use the names of real people and not just generic ones like "politicians" or "millionaires." However, if this is an overarching plan, and the first time you are putting one together, go ahead and work in generalities. Attached with each name, compose a list of messages that you will use to reach out to each of them. The messages might be similar for each group. Also come up with a list of recommended strategies for getting these messages out to the people you are trying to reach. By that, I mean are you going to use an e-mail campaign, are you going to create posters and place them in your community, are you going to hold public forums? It is a really good idea to do these in list form like this:

Public: Mayor Miles A. Whey
Message: We need more stop signs near our local schools because people are driving too fast in school zones.
Strategy: E-mails, postcards and phone calls. Hold community forums to discuss safety.

Calendar: When developing any kind of plan, whether short term or long range, you really need to know when things need to get done. You need to have it all written down.

Budget: It is really important that you put in writing how much money, if any, that you are willing and able to dedicate to this project. It is also really important that you stick to that number. It is okay to spend under the amount you set aside, but never spend over that amount.

Evaluation – It is always good that you evaluate any plan you create. Of course, you cannot evaluate something until you have done it. So in this section you should write out HOW you will evaluate your plan in order to determine if it worked or not. Figure out how you will determine if you have succeeded. This will provide you with an opportunity to redirect your course of action.

Now, as I have stressed several times throughout this book, if you have the means to hire a communications professional to do this for you, then I would suggest you do so. If you do not have the means, and that is why you bought and are reading this book, then go ahead and start planning. You will learn a great deal through this process. This will be your strategic communications plan that you created. There is a great deal of personal satisfaction that can come from that.

Okay, now grab a pencil and develop YOUR Communications

Plan Checklist:

- ✓ What is the issue?
- ✓ What is the solution?
- ✓ Who can help you create change?
- ✓ Who needs to be mobilized?

Thing 5

Be Proactive

Managing Media Effectively

Effective media management can go a long way toward reducing your on-the-job headaches. It will take a little time, and practice, but with proper planning you can learn to deal with the media and effectively cultivate good press contacts.

Throughout all of your planning you have to be flexible and learn to **"go with the flow."** Does that sound familiar? It's important to have some kind of a plan. However, things don't always go as planned and a reporter's deadline will not always mirror when you are ready, able and available to release information. Flexibility is one key to success with the press.

It's also important to remember that **there are no permanent friends or enemies in the media.** One day, a reporter does a positive story involving your business or organization and the next story could be negative. Keep an even keel! Despite what many anti-press pundits would like you to believe, the media is not always out to "get you" or unearth a controversy. The majority of reporters are overworked people who just want to make their deadlines, do their jobs well and go home at the end of the day.

Media coverage can help you meet strategic objectives. Not every story done about your school, business or organization is going to be positive, but if you can be proactive you have a better chance of turning the tide in your favor.

It's important that you be proactive in your approach to media management. If you own a small or medium sized business or run a nonprofit organization you know that things are not going to get done unless you do it yourself. The same can be said for media management. It's up to you to watch the news, read your local newspapers and listen to the radio. Pay attention to the hot topics of the moment. If an issue arises that possibly impacts your profession or cause then you should consider calling the local news folks and offering your input.

For example, once when I was a television reporter in Dallas, we were in the grips of a nasty drought. Of course, droughts are really nothing new in Texas, but I digress. At the time, the local governments warned people against excessive watering of their lawns and gardens. People faced fines for using too much water or letting their sprinklers run too long. While in the newsroom one day, I picked up the phone and on the other end of the line was a fellow from a landscaping company who began talking about what people can do to keep their lawns and gardens alive during dry times, without using too much water and getting themselves in hot water. (Pun intended.)

The light bulb went off in my head. I saw a story here, mainly because this guy had the foresight to call.

ME: "Would you consider helping us with a story telling people some of the ways that they can take care of their grass and flowers without getting into trouble?"

CALLER: "Sure, what time can you be here?"

Later that day the man's company was featured in a story on the evening news. While I did not do any follow up research regarding the impact of his call (I did not know then that I would be writing this book) I am sure that he received calls from prospective customers who began their conversations with the words: "I saw your company on TV and I was wondering…"

Now, at this point you might take a hard look at that scenario I just described and point out that the guy from the landscaping company used me and that he pulled one over on me to get on television. For the most part that's sort of true. But we each got something out of it; he got some free advertising by opening his doors to a television crew, and I got a good story for the evening news. We both won!

As a company or organization you can use the current news of the day to your advantage, whether that news is good or bad. If there is a string of nasty muggings in your community and you run a karate school, call the local media and offer to provide self-defense tips to the public at some type of community forum. If you read the newspapers and see that the government is considering limiting the tax breaks on big-ticket items and you run a tax preparation firm, consider calling your local media and offering yourself as a resource to tell people about the new laws and how they will impact people. There are countless ways to proactively participate in news coverage that will produce positive results.

The media educates the public and influences public opinion. Remember the great quote from CBS News icon Edward R. Murrow: "Television can inform, it can educate, it can inspire. But only to the extent that it is used for these purposes-- otherwise it's only lights and wires in a box."

By now, just about everyone understands the power of the media, especially television. Murrow was one of the first to understand – or at least publicly state – that television and the media in general, is a powerful educational tool. And if you are hoping to cultivate a meaningful relationship with your local media then you must understand that the media can help you educate the public (a.k.a. consumers, potential customers, the general public) about what your company or organization is all about.

You have the power – through the media – to educate and if you can educate people then you can have some impact on public opinion. In addition to having some impact on public opinion, you can also help inform the public about what your group, organization or company does. And to think you learned it after reading this book! It gives me goose bumps!

Thing 6

Determine WHO You Are Trying to Reach

Target Audiences

**Parents - Students - Politicians – Community Leaders –
Business Owners - New   Customers – Old Customers**

We briefly touched on this a little earlier. It's important that you determine your target audience – who do you want to reach with your message? Why do you want to reach them? It could be any group of people.   Basically, it's usually one of the following groups:

- Parents
- Students
- Politicians
- Community Leaders
- Business Owners
- New Customers
- Old Customers

Think about exactly who it is that you are trying to reach. Put together a list of your target audiences. The list does not have to be in order of importance.

1)

2)

3)

4)

5)

How can you take aim at your target if you do not know what your target is? It is important that you go about all of this in a strategic manner. You do not want to be spinning your wheels because your time is limited and valuable.

If you don't figure out ahead of time exactly who it is that you are trying to reach then you will find yourself wasting a lot of time reaching out to the wrong groups. You need to find new customers. You need to rally people to your cause. You really need to increase donations to your nonprofit organization in order to survive.

Don't waste your time because your time is precious.

Thing 7

Determine What Separates YOU
from the Others

I don't think I am being rude when I say that while your group or company is pretty special that there are dozens like yours listed in the phonebook or easily found through a Google search. I think you know that. So, as you set sail in your media relations journey in search of media contacts, what can you tell them that makes you or your group so special and worthy of valuable news time, or space if we are talking about a newspaper?

Competition is crazy out there. Nonprofits are battling with each other for those donations that seem to be decreasing by the day. Businesses are struggling everywhere and are scratching for every dollar they can. More and more people seem to have less and less time these days to volunteer with a community group. So, what makes your organization so special anyway?

If you cannot answer that question, you need to start thinking of an answer. It is really important that you have at the ready a list of reasons why you are more deserving than others for media attention, for donations, for new members.

It is important that you know why you want to educate the public about who you are and what you do. What's important about your group, organization or business?

Create a list of ten things that separates you from the others.

1)

2)

3)

4)

5)

6)

7)

8)

9)

10)

In fact, it would be a good idea if you took the list you just created and placed it somewhere prominently in your office for everyone to see. You want everyone to know what makes your group so special and what separates you from the others.

Thing 8

Some simple ways to introduce YOURSELF to the media

Media/Public Outreach Tips

How to reach out and make contact with the media...

Here are a few media relations and public outreach tips that can help you get your message out to the general public or just help publicize some of the great programs your office/organization has to offer people:

- Organize **media tours** of your programs and services. Invite groups of reporters, local bloggers and community leaders to visit your organization or operation. This allows visitors to observe first-hand what you do.

- Hold **"open house"** receptions to profile specific programs that are worthy of showcasing.

- Host **community luncheons** and invite business leaders, community leaders, local politicians, social service organization leaders, members of the media. In this type of informal setting, you can meet and begin to develop contacts with media representatives. If you don't have much of a budget make them "brown bag" lunches where people bring their own food.

- Invite editorial writers to **visit programs** that deserve to be highlighted, or programs you'd like to promote.

- **Establishing contact** with editorial writers – who can be very influential - gives you the opportunity to showcase programs.

- Launch **letter writing campaigns** to local newspapers, legislators, praising the benefits of whatever programs you wish to promote. This can sometimes spark interest from newspapers, which could lead to stories in the local paper. At the very least, this can begin to establish contact with media representatives.

- **Hold community forums and public meetings** in conjunction with local PTA meetings, school boards, or scouts or wherever your request to appear can be accepted. This also provides you with the opportunity to highlight what you do.

- **Submit guest editorials**. Many community newspapers accept guest editorial submissions from people in the local community. This offers you a great opportunity to offer opinions, tell people what you are up to, and brag about your group or organization.

Thing 9

Realize That Media Relations Is WORK and <u>Not</u> MAGIC

What a media relations plan CAN'T do for you

Don't expect overnight miracles...

There are a lot of things that having a media relations plan can do for you and your group, organization or business. It can raise your visibility and maybe even your bottom line if you are into that money-making thing. It can help improve your position in your local community. However, you need to understand that there are a lot of things that media relations **cannot** do for you. You have to understand that miracles will not happen overnight.

So, it's time for a brief reality check. Here is a short list of things that media relations planning **CAN'T** do for you:

Immediately thrust you into the spotlight: Building a good media relations plan is like building the foundation of a home. It has to be solid and it takes time to create one properly. If you follow the suggestions laid out in this book you will be able to start building a nice, solid communications foundation. However, you cannot expect that once you've got your ideas down on paper, and your assignments handed out to staff, and your media contact list cobbled together that all of these elements will automatically thrust you into the media spotlight. Realistically, that will take time... and patience... and maybe even more patience. The good news is that you are well on your way to achieving your communications goals by taking the steps that you are taking.

Control the media and the message: The old saying goes "You can lead a horse to water but you can't make him drink." In the case of media you could say "You can lead reporters to a story but you can't make them report the story the way that you want, if they report it at all." You don't have any control over the story that will be reported about you. All that you can control is the information that you provide to reporters. That's it. You don't have editorial control over what news stations and newspapers report. It can definitely be frustrating but try not to agonize over it. Also, be careful if you decide to put up a fight. If a reporter covers your story and makes glaring errors, then you are within your rights to lodge a complaint with that reporter's superiors. If that reporter missed some obvious facts and decided to editorialize rather than report the news, then you also have some room to complain. However, if you just didn't like the way the reporter covered the story, or if the paper published an unflattering photo of you, then there's not much that you can do about that.

Do away with negatives: Media relations will not eliminate negatives. Having a well thought out media relations plan will not make negatives go away. Negatives get reported. There's no way around that. If you are part of a news story involving some type of program or process, there is always the possibility that some negatives will be brought up in the story: an organization with a different motive says something negative about your efforts, a former staff member might offer a disparaging quote, or a public official might take a verbal swipe at you. There's not much that you can do about that, except respond politely and professionally. Bad news is bad news and having a media relations plan in place will not make a bad story better. If something has put your business or program in a bad light, media relations won't eliminate the negatives being reported. However, keep in mind that media relations planning can help accentuate the positives that you do wish to highlight.

Do away with the competition: There are probably a lot of folks out there that do what you do, whether it's a business, a nonprofit organization or a community group. That is just a fact of life. Face the fact that there are other organizations out there providing the same service, maybe in similar fashion to the way that you do it. Having a media plan of some sort will not make those competitors go away. However, having some kind of plan will hopefully bring you more positive attention than the others.

Automatically give you credibility: Having a communications plan in place will not make you an instant expert in the eyes of reporters and editors. It will not guarantee you goodwill automatically. What it can and will do is help you open the door to gaining the kind of notoriety that you want and need to succeed. You will not have instant credibility moments after developing and implementing your media relations plan, but you will find yourself steps ahead of your competitors.

Thing 10
Define YOUR Issues

Figuring Out What Is Important to You

- Identify the issues that affect, concern or influence the members of your audience(s)
- Determine the pros and cons
- Every activity must have a purpose

It's also important that you clearly identify and define your issues – the issues that serve as the main focus of whatever project you are focusing on. It seems like this part would be easy, but if you really sit down and spend some time, you will find out that it is more challenging than you realize.

While you might have done this earlier in the process, this is really the time to refine and elaborate on what you are doing and what you are trying to accomplish. The issue or issues that you have identified will form the foundation of your project.

Now that you have identified your target audience, you need to **identify the issues that affect, concern, or influence** the members of these groups. Many times different groups or organizations are interested in the same causes and issues. This gives you the opportunity to work together. Remember, there's strength in numbers. Later on, as you learn about writing news releases and setting up press conferences, this information will come in handy to you when you are trying to convey a united front to the public.

Also take some time to determine the **pros and cons** of the issues you have identified as you are connecting them with your target audience. This will help you have better control over who is part of the group that you will later present at future events that you are planning: forums, press conferences, and public meetings.

So, maybe as a group exercise with other folks in your organization, get together and identify your issues:

1)

2)

3)

4)

5)

6)

7)

8)

9)

10)

If it turns out that your list of issues is a lengthy one, then it would definitely be a good idea to team up with other organizations when working with the media on certain issues. You might find out that you share the same interests and issues with other groups that are seeking the same results.

All of this pre-planning will make a lot more sense as you move through the media relations planning process. As I mentioned earlier, think of building a communications plan as if it is like building a house. Right now, you are beginning to lay down the foundation and you really want your foundation to be a solid one.

Thing 11

Define YOUR Style

You Really Must Determine Your Approach

- Proactive or reactive?
- Publicly or behind the scenes?
- One approach or multiple approaches?
- Focus on any one issue more?

Once you've determined your issue, you need to determine how to approach it.

Do you need to be **proactive** or **reactive** in dealing with the media? Is this a situation where you want to set the tone and speak up first, or wait and react to something that's happened?

If you have the choice, it would be best if you chose "proactive" because being proactive helps you set the tone for the story and it gives you more control. If you are reaching out to a reporter or some other news executive then you have the opportunity to tell your side of the story first. And there's a great advantage to getting your side of the story out first. It can become YOUR story.

Do you need to be **very public** or work privately **behind the scenes**? Either way is effective and either way involves some planning. Working behind the scenes to make media connections and persuade news operations to do stories about you and your organization actually requires more work than working "wide out in the open" because it takes time to build issue related relationships and coalitions.

For instance, let's suppose that you are a small shop owner working along a busy street that is in need of better traffic control. Cars speed along too fast and customers fear that it's not safe to frequent your shop or the ones near yours. You've gone to your local traffic planners for help but have not received the results you want. So, you have two options to consider; first, you can work behind the scenes, going from fellow merchant to fellow merchant coaxing each one of them to contact the media individually about your traffic problem. This will take a lot of time and might not provide good results. Your fellow merchants might start contacting local media outlets at different times over a prolonged period of time. Stringing the calls out to reporters might prompt them to lose interest rather than gain interest.

Another good approach is to send e-mails to reporters or editors to convince them of the validity of your cause. Newspaper and news station websites usually have the individual e-mail addresses of reporters. Those addresses are easy to find. Find them. Send these reporters messages explaining the reason why you believe your story is important. If we are still following our "too fast traffic on the street in front of our stores" example, send the media photos, or even short video clips, of the speeding traffic, or post the video on your Facebook page or on YouTube (we will talk about these sites a little later). That approach could really help get the media's attention. At the very least, it could help bring attention to your cause.

Actually, working publicly might work to your advantage better. When contacting your fellow merchants find out what day would be good for each of them to take part in a news conference where – as a group – your will be bringing your issues and concerns to the media. (You'll learn later on about organizing and arranging press conferences.)

Will **one approach** work for all audiences or will you need **multiple approaches**? As we discussed just a few sentences ago, there's no "one size fits all" approach when it comes to media relations.

Will you need to focus on any one issue more than another? The answer to that question is most likely a resounding YES.

More than likely, you will have to multi-task and deal with multiple issues at one time. Proper planning will help you better handle this.

Make a List of the Pros and Cons

  ✓ Should we be proactive or reactive?

  ✓ Should we act publicly or behind the scenes?

  ✓ Should we use one approach or multiple approaches?

  ✓ Should we focus on more than one issue?

  ✓ Should we work individually, or as a group?

When you first begin making your pros and cons list, do not be afraid to make it long and elaborate. You always can go back later and trim it down to make it more manageable. At least for the very beginning, the longer the better.

Thing 12

Figure Out What You Want to Say
and Who will Say it

Creating Your Key Messages

- Talking Points to help you communicate
- Brief memorable sentences
- Expressions, slogans or words

Key messages are **talking points** or **message points** that you will be using to communicate with your target audience. These are important to have, important to keep, and vitally important to commit to memory.

These are **brief, easy to remember sentences** and phrases that are designed to stick in people's minds. Let's do a little experiment right now using the Internet. I hate to say this but put this book down for just a few minutes. Go over to your computer and do a search using the term "key message points." You'll find millions of results from just about any organization that you can think of: universities, businesses, sports teams, associations, politicians.

Key messages are an integral part of any media related campaign.

These are **expressions, slogans** or even individual **words** used to help you express your bottom line. Most slogans are associated with major corporations. Adidas says "Impossible is nothing." Fed-Ex is known for "When it absolutely, positively has to be there overnight." Coca-Cola says "It's the real thing." Raid "Kills bugs dead." Allstate says "You're in good hands."

There's no reason why a local business or community group can't have a meaningful and catchy slogan of its own. However, as you are developing your campaign or media outreach program, keep simple words and phrases in mind as you are massaging your message. What you say might not catch fire with the public, but by reinforcing over and over again the points you are trying to stress to the press, those words and phrases will become synonymous with your efforts.

Here are some examples of message points that have no connections with each other but are the types of phrases that you can create and commit to memory when making contact with the media:

- Our staff is trained and ready to accomplish this mission. We are committed to this cause and want the public to know that.
- The Mayor's proposals are ambitious. However, we feel they fall short of protecting the small business owner, the people who are the backbone of our local economy.
- We had hoped the Governor's budget would have taken into account what small, nonprofit organizations like ours mean to their local communities.
- As an organization, we would support a local tax increase if we felt the money would be used to help more people.

You get the idea.

Sometimes speakers are able to memorize the talking points they are using, but you must make sure that what you are saying does not sound too rehearsed. You don't want to seem robotic. In many cases, it works just as well to concentrate on using key words and phrases that can help you make your point.

The key to developing and using key messages is to make sure that what you are saying is clear and understandable. You don't want anything that you say to create mixed messages, or sound as if they have double meaning. In most cases, straight talk should produce straight results.

Paul Sanchez is the global director of employee research for Mercer Human Resource Consulting. In the May 2006 issue of CFO Magazine he said something very important regarding message: "The first and most important thing is to have a clear understanding about the importance of communicating comprehensively, promptly, with as much transparency as is possible."

Translation: communicate clearly and people will hear you.

Develop Your Message Points

Develop a List of Key Messages or Phrases Representing Your Organization or Mission

1)

2)

3)

4)

5)

6)

7)

8)

9)

10)

Selecting a Spokesperson

Now that you have figured out what it is that you want to say, who will speak for your group?

The Merriam-Webster dictionary defines a spokesperson as "a person who speaks as the representative of another or others in a professional capacity." Pretty much every company, especially the large ones, has a spokesperson of some type. Some organizations have gone to great lengths to select the right person, while other groups just pick a warm body who can string a few coherent sentences together. (I would not recommend that option and soon will explain further.)

Interviews can be intimidating, even for those with a lot of media experience. A spokesperson must know how to articulate the "company line" for lack of a better phrase. Whoever is chosen as your spokesperson must know how to advance your organization's goals, viewpoints and objectives. The person chosen for this role has a lot of responsibility because the media's power cannot be ignored and sometimes you only get one shot and representing who you are and what you do. You have to get it right.

One of the first questions you might ask is "how important is it that we even think of having an official spokesperson? Is communications really that important?" Well, communications is a big deal and it's getting bigger. According to a survey of CEOs by *PR Week*/Burson-Marsteller, 75-percent of the respondents stated that they are spending more time and effort communicating with customers and 64-percent said they are now spending more time with the media than ever before. Increased visibility is driving the need for more and better communications, which is driving the need for good spokespeople to represent you and your group or organization.

So, how do you go about selecting a spokesperson and why should you select one in the first place? Let's answer the second question first. You need to select a spokesperson because you need one person to handle media inquiries and to make inquiries to the media. You need one representative with whom the media, and eventually the public, can identify. You also don't want several people handling media inquiries because you want to speak with a consistent voice, and you don't want several people doing the same job. As we all know, the left hand and the right hand don't always communicate. It's important that you have stability in the communications area.

Now, there are several things to consider when selecting someone to serve as your group's spokesperson:

- That person must be articulate and well-spoken.
- That person must convey trust and credibility.
- He/she must appear to be genuine and sincere.
- A good spokesperson is good at thinking quickly on his/her feet.
- Even though you might be "the boss" your organization's spokesperson might not necessarily be YOU.

That last bullet may hurt your feelings, but you have to face the truth. Perhaps you are a wonderful leader and a personable guy or gal with a brilliant business mind, but maybe you are not the right one to serve as the spokesperson. Take a good, hard look at yourself to determine if you can "represent well" if called upon to answer questions from the media. Ask those who work for you, or with you, if they feel that you could handle the task. Don't get upset if they respond to you honestly and you don't like what they are telling you. Insist that they be honest, and tell you if you are not the right guy for the job. If they tell you that they believe someone else should speak for the group, then accept their judgment gracefully and find the right person who will represent the organization well. You will still be heavily involved in the crafting of the "company message." You just won't be the person who delivers that message.

Not everyone can be a spokesperson. If you are going to go through the effort to find someone, one of the best things you can do (if you have the money) is have that person professionally trained. If you have the money to do it, it is money well spent.

Media training is taken very seriously in the world of big business. According to a survey by Impulse Research, nine out of ten CEOs have had some sort of formal media training. Why do so many corporate bosses going through media training? Nearly 84-percent of those CEOs questioned for the same survey said media interviews were the most effective way to get their message across.

Spokespeople are popping up just about everywhere. Several years ago, the Xinhua News Agency reported that spokesperson training programs were not keeping up with the demand of local governments in China. That's right in CHINA! The State Council Information Office has been training hundreds of spokespeople from central departments and provincial governments because of the increasing interest in information there.

China put the new training to use during the spread of SARS (Severe Acute Respiratory Syndrome). China developed a health matter reporting system and a news release system featuring the use of spokespeople. So, if the spokesperson concept can work in China, it can work for your organization, and while you might not like what the Chinese government says or does, you have to admire the preparedness, even if you don't like the results.

So, depending on the size of your budget, consider professional media training for you and your spokesperson. It's a worthy investment. There are plenty of good, reputable companies out there that specialize in media training. If you don't have the money for professional training then there are some simple and inexpensive ways to practice and prepare yourself.

- Make sure staff knows that you (or your designated spokesperson) will be handling all calls from the media from now on. Tell them to NOT answer press questions themselves.
- Think of questions you'd most likely be asked by reporters and practice your answers.
- Develop a standard set of "message points" about your group, organization or company. Have them handy or have them memorized.
- Set up a mock news conference and have staff ask you questions.
- Videotape your mock press conferences to see how you performed. Ask staff members to watch the video replay with you and offer brutally honest critiques.
- Take your practicing seriously by watching how others handle the task. Watch televised news conferences to see how interview subjects are handling the questions and the pressure.
- Practice and plan.

Remember, there is power in preparation. The better prepared you are – or your spokesperson is – the better your group, organization or company will look when the press comes calling.

Who Is Your Spokesperson?

List the People within Your Group/Organization and Their Strong Points Which Would Make Them Good Spokespeople

1)

2)

3)

4)

5)

Thing 13

Build a Media Relations "TOOLKIT"

What Makes Up a Media Relations "Toolkit"?

Media Statements — Background Papers– Position Papers — Fact Sheets– Brochures– Q&A Sheets — Fliers — Memos

Any handyman worth his salt would not think of looking over a potential project without bringing with him his trusty toolkit. Having a good media relations plan requires that you also have a collection of tools to get the job done properly. The following is a list of some of the most common tools:

Media statements: These are kind of like the message points that we addressed earlier, but they are more extensive. In addition to having really short and memorable phrases, you also should have longer messages containing quotes that you can deliver to the press. These are things that you should have on file or committed to memory that you can "deliver" at a moment's notice. Media statements can also be specific and geared toward a particular subject or issue. In those types of cases, you will have to take particular care in crafting them to make sure you are transmitting the right "messages".

Background papers: These give a little history about your organization or the topic of interest, depending on the subject matter. It's a good idea to have these on file, or even on display at your reception desk, if you have one. When someone comes to your office and asks "Can you tell me a little more about what you do?" you will have something ready to hand out. Background papers also come in handy when you are putting together folders to pass out to reporters, and the general public, at news conferences that you might hold. Think of these as being like bios, only they are not about you, they are about your organization.

Position Papers: These describe your stance on specific issues and are fairly simple to write. They basically address how you or your group might stand on a certain issue. These are fairly brief and get to the point. Consider these as being similar to editorial columns, like the ones you read in the newspaper. These come in particularly handy if your organization becomes involved in some sort of controversial issue and your group is either for it or against it. Having a position paper ready to hand out to the media lets reporters know your stance right away.

Q & A Sheets: These are common questions and answers that are pertinent to the topic at hand. If you check the Web sites of other companies and organizations you will see that many of them have a FAQ (Frequently Asked Questions) section. Create an FAQ sheet of your own, even if the questions you come up with are not "frequently asked" by the general public this will give you an opportunity to let people know more about who you are and what you do.

Brochures: These are advertisement types of documents that help promote or explain whatever program or event you are highlighting. Chances are you have samples lying around and don't even realize it. You can always "model" your brochure after a sample you might admire, and you can even use some off-the-shelf computer design program to create your own brochure. If you have the money in your budget, it's always good to consider hiring a professional graphic designer to create a brochure for you. Sometimes it's best NOT to have your brochure look too "home made." However, if you are looking for ways to cut costs, designing your own brochure will cost you much less than it would if you hired a designer.

Fliers: These are basic advertisements or explainers of upcoming events or programs. You see them everywhere, on store counters, on the windshield of your car when you've been in a shopping center parking lot for a while. Again, you can also create these things yourself or hire a professional to do the job.

Memos: If you have any of these that are pertinent to a particular issue, you can use these along with background papers to emphasize the stance you've taken on certain issues. Of course, please make sure that the memos you plan on using don't contain any confidential material.

Videos: Producing videos to accompany your cause can go a long way to helping you make whatever point it is you are trying to make. When you get a chance, go online and look at some of the videos that have been produced by companies wanting to not only tell people, but SHOW people who they are and what they do. Once again, without risking like sounding like a broken record, hire a professional production person to do your video if you have the means. Nothing looks worse than a cheesy looking image video, unless that's the kind of image that you'd like to project. These videos are perfect for posting on your website or on your Facebook and if you want to include them in your "toolbox" burn a copy of your video(s) onto a DVD and include them in a press packet.

Press clippings from previous news coverage: Putting old newspapers clippings in a press kit can serve as evidence that your topic is newsworthy, or that your group is credible. This lets people know that you are not a "media rookie" even though you might be one. It also lets people know that you have been the subject of media stories or interviews in the past. Don't forget that when you think of press clippings, also think about any coverage you might have had on any of the smaller, community news websites that might serve your area. It also helps if those clippings are positive in some way, or show your organization in a good light. That goes without saying.

Media Relations Toolkit Checklist

Do You Have Any or All of the Following? If you do, then list them.

If not, begin developing them...

- ✓ Media statements?

- ✓ Background papers?

- ✓ Position Papers?

- ✓ Q & A Sheets?

- ✓ Brochures?

- ✓ Fliers?

- ✓ Memos?

- ✓ Videos? :

- ✓ Press clippings from previous news coverage?

Thing 14

Learn to Write News Releases and Media Advisories

The Press Release

- Who
- What
- When
- Where
- Why

The American Heritage Dictionary describes a news release as "an announcement of an event, performance, or other newsworthy item that is issued to the press." Seems like a simple definition. But are news releases simple to write? Well, the first few that you write might be a little tough but after a while you'll get the hang of it.

The most important information in the news release has to go first. It's the old: who, what, when, where and why information.

The first paragraph of your release sets the tone for the rest of the release. Try not to make your releases too long. You might have the desire to load them up with all the pertinent information, but a lot of it ends up being ignored. Avoid that desire and just go with the basic information. Reporters should always ask for additional information at your events, the ones they are drawn to by your wonderfully crafted release. If they don't ask for additional info when the time comes, then GIVE IT TO THEM ANY WAY.

Remember to put your releases on official letterhead, or displaying an official logo. This lets the media know the source of the information right away.

Include your contact information: phone numbers, cell phone numbers, e-mail addresses and Web site addresses. This type of information is important because reporters and assignment editors for newspapers or radio and television stations might have a few questions they'd like to ask you first before deciding whether to cover your event.

The date of release is important. It'll mostly be "For Immediate Release." That lets reporters know the event is happening soon or that the issue deserves attention **now**. Include the current date or the day you are releasing the information. Sometimes releases will sit on an editor's desk unless the date is prominent.

A grabbing headline is important. Without one you won't get attention. For example, if you were a reporter would you cover an event after receiving a news release with a headline reading: "Nortel Achieves 3.6 Megabits Per Second HSDPA Data Call With Qualcomm"? Probably not because the headline makes no sense, except maybe to the highest of high tech geeks. Well, to be honest, that was an actual press release headline, and you wonder if the story got any attention as a result. Perhaps a headline like this would have worked better: "Nortel and Qualcomm Team Up to Make Cell Phones Faster."

It's maybe not great, but it's makes a little more sense. And remember, making sense is important.

Quote the important partners in your release to add more legitimacy to what you are doing. Keep the quotes brief. Quotes also add weight and authority to your release.

If you have volumes of background material then place it on pages separate from the news release. If you have minimal background information then sprinkle it throughout your release to make it read like a newspaper story.

Keep reading and you'll find a sample press release that you can use as a guide. Or better yet, search on the Internet for "sample press releases" and you'll find tons of examples that you can use.

Important Press Release Ingredients

What to add to make it work...

Like a good recipe, news releases have important ingredients.

Be descriptive with what you are writing. This will better explain your event or issue. Avoid being vague. Vagueness will cause media disinterest.

Personalize your message. Make it have meaning for the intended audience. Try something like this: "For young parents in the district.." or "If your child needs tutoring…"

Localize your release in order to localize your story. That should be obvious. It's all about local. Local people go to local stores. Local people donate to local organizations doing good things in the community.

Summarize your quotes in "sound bites." Try to keep the quotes that you put in news releases succinct and to the point. If they are long and wordy they will look as if they were written quotes and not spoken ones. People will not find your story interesting if they find your quotes uninteresting.

Finally, maintain your message. Don't stray. Make sure that each line in your release supports your message. When in doubt – remove it.

Remember: a well-written and well-received news release can reap great rewards for your company, organization or group. News releases - sometimes also called press releases - are a staple of any communications/public relations effort. Learning to write them and use them properly will go a long way to helping you spread your message.

Important Elements

The "Human Face"- Visuals & Symbols—Media Soundbites

Important things to remember when crafting news releases:

- The best stories have a "human face." Viewers/readers need to identify with someone in order for the story to have meaning for them. Make sure that real people are involved with your story.
- Make the story easy to cover for reporters. Try keeping the event at one place, if possible. Provide background material. (Remember, we talked about background material just a few pages ago.) Have interview subjects prepared to talk.
- Cater to the local media. A mention in USA Today is nice but you really want the local paper or the Neighbors section of your larger metropolitan paper to cover you. It's what your community reads.
- Explain why your event is newsworthy. Educate the reporter on the issue if necessary.
- Ride the coattails of current events: NASA launches a big satellite into space, tie it to a big science fair. If it's an election year, stage some kind of civics event, like a mock election or a student debate.
- Visuals and symbols are important. If you are involved in a story that involves schools and children, the press conference you have on a playground with kids in the background says more than the one in the office at your desk.
- Speaking in media bites improves your chances of being quoted... and quoted correctly. Long quotes force reporters to take long notes. That improves the chances of you being misquoted or **not** quoted at all.

Other Press Release Tools

Other ways to get your stories out to the press...

In addition to written and individual press releases, there are several other press release tools at your disposal.

Media advisories are one-page reminders sent out to the press usually the day before an event... also before or after the press release goes out. (An example is coming shortly. Be patient!)

Backgrounders are one or two pages you can make available that can give the history or a certain event or program without trying to cram all of that information into a press release. These are briefer than background papers that we discussed earlier. They can be written in bullet point form to make them easier to read.

Press Packets are given out at press conferences – or meetings. They contain press releases, backgrounders, bios, program information and all of the other things we've discussed in the previous pages. Use whatever materials that you want to include.

Word of caution: If you make a press packet too big you risk the possibility that most of the information will be tossed out by reporters. Reporters have limited time to deal with constant deadlines. In many cases, reporters don't have a great deal of time to sift through stacks of paperwork no matter how vital you think the information is to telling your story to the world.

Sample Press Release

FOR IMMEDIATE RELEASE:

CONTACT:
Your Name
Your Company's Name
Phone Number/Cell Number
FAX Number
Email Address
Website Address

Your Company Makes a Big Announcement (Put snappy headline here)

Your headline must grab the attention of the editor. It should be in bold type and a font that is larger than the body text. Preferred type fonts are Arial, Times New Roman, or Verdana. Keep the headline brief and capitalize every word with the exception of "a", "the" "an" or any word that is three characters or less.

<City>, <State>, <Date> - The first paragraph of your release should be written in a clear and concise manner. The opening sentence contains the most important information; keep it to 25 words or less. Never take for granted that the reader has read your headline. It needs contain information that will "attract" the reader. Remember, your story must be newsworthy and factual; don't make it a sales pitch or it will end up as a coaster under someone's coffee cup.

Don't forget to answer "who", "what", "when", "where", "why" and "how". Your text should include relevant information about your product, service or event. If writing about a product, make sure to include details on when the product is available, where it can be purchased and how much it costs. If you're writing about an event, include the date, location of the event and any other pertinent information.

Don't forget to include a quote from someone that is a credible source of information; include their title or position with the company, and why they are a credible source.

Keep your sentences and paragraphs short; a paragraph should be no more than 3-4 sentences. Your release should be brief, between 500 to 800 words, written in a word processing program, and spell checked for errors.

Watch for grammatical errors. Proofread the thing! The mood of the release should be factual. Don't hype anything or you will be ignored! Sales pitches will ruin your credibility with the reader.

The last paragraph before the company information should read: For additional information on (put in the subject of this release), contact "name" or visit www.yoururl.com. If you offer a sample, copy or demo, put the information in here. You can also include details on product availability, trademark acknowledgment, etc. in this area of the release.

ABOUT <COMPANY> - Include a brief description of your company along with the products and services it provides.

- END – or - ###

At the end of the release, you need to indicate that the release is ended. This lets the journalists know they have received the entire release. Type "End" or type "###" on the first line after your text is completed. If your release goes over one page, type "MORE" at the bottom of the first page.

You've got the tools. Write your release!

Media Distribution List

You need to develop a database of media contacts...

Before you begin sending out media advisories and press releases you need to figure out to whom and where you are going to send them. You don't want to go flailing around in the dark as you start distributing your information. What this means is that you are going to have to build some kind of list and maybe even create a database. This is going to take time and effort on your part, or on the part of a member of your staff. But, in the long run, it will be worth it.

In assembling your media contact list, figure out which journalists working for your local media outlets - print, radio, TV & online - cover your geographic area, which ones might specialize in your industry, or handle topics pertinent to you and what you do.

This is the information you want to include in your database:

- Name
- Media Outlet
- Address
- Phone Number
- Fax Number (Yes, some agencies still use fax machines!)
- E-mail address

You might even want to get more specific by including information like publication deadlines, ongoing special features that certain reporters might cover, secondary contacts within the same organizations and things of this nature.

If you don't have the time to create a mailing list there are always places where you can purchase them. That might save you time but you run the risk that the information you are purchasing is out of date. You might be better off creating your own list.

It's important that you make these exploratory calls yourself in order to help you develop a short list of contacts. This will enable you to find out key journalists' interests, deadlines, and how they prefer to receive information. This will also give them the chance to learn something about you and your group or organization. Consider it an important first step toward building strong relationships with media contacts!

Sample Media Advisory

Media Advisory

Put the main headline here to grab the editor's attention

The Sub-Headline Goes Here and It Includes Additional Information in Italics

CITY OR COMPANY NAME CAN GO HERE – This is where you write a brief paragraph or two to tell the editors what you are advising them about and why you want them to care. Remember, this is not a press release where you really have to pack in a bunch of facts. You can just include the basics to advise people about an upcoming event, the release of a study, a scheduled press conference, a community rally, or whatever you have scheduled.

Unlike a press release, you don't have to write "For Immediate Release" on advisories because you are just giving the media a "heads up" about something down the road. Editors put media advisories in their files for future reference.

WHO: Tell who you are, what groups and people will be attending

WHAT: **Presentation, Press Conference, Rally, etc.**

WHERE: **Give the exact location down to the zip code and room number of your event**

WHEN: **Day, Date, Time**

This would be a good place to provide editors with the names of all the individuals associated with your group or organization who will be available for individual interviews before, during, or after your event.

Contact:
Your Name
Your Title
Your Company/Group/Organization
Your phone numbers both desk and cell
Your e-mail address
Your web site – if you have one

About You
This is the perfect place to put a little background information about your company/group/organization. Keep it to a brief, one-paragraph description of who you are and what you do. If you write something too long it will go unnoticed. Also, remember to include your Web site address – if you have a site – so editors can do a little background checking on their own to decide whether you are legitimate or not. Don't forget to include the media advisory and press release on your Web site if there is an appropriate place there.

You've got the tools. Write your advisory!

Create Your Media Distribution List

Jot Down a List of Media Organizations in Your Coverage Area.

When putting together your list also consider small newspapers that only publish once or twice a week as well as your normal larger newspapers.

1)

2)

3)

4)

5)

6)

7)

8)

9)

10)

A Final Word about News Releases and Media Advisories

One thing to keep in mind is that you should not just think of the media as being the recipient of your finely crafted news releases. You should also post them on your company or organization's website. Create a "news" section on the site where you can post your releases. This will give reporters, and the general public, a place to go to find out more information about you or your group. In addition to posting these news releases on your site, you also can distribute them via e-mail to the people on your mailing list. This is a great way to keep your stakeholders informed about what is going on within your organization. Think of it this way: News releases are NOT just for the news media anymore!

Thing 15

Learn How to Sell YOURSELF

The Phone Pitch

Making the cold call...

Let's face it; no one really likes making the "cold call." For those of you who are not salespeople I am referring to the unsolicited call out of the blue from one party to another where the caller tries getting the recipient interested in something that they might not know anything about. They're not a lot of fun to make and they're often difficult, unless you have telemarketing experience. However, cold calls are important if you are trying to pitch a story idea to a reporter or editor. It might not be pleasant, but it's a survival skill worth learning.

Do your research before calling a reporter or editor. News organizations often post contact names and numbers on their Web sites. You'll often find the information online. Most newspapers now not only include the byline of the reporter who wrote a particular story, by also that reporter's e-mail address. If the information you need is not online there's always the phonebook, or call directory assistance as a last resort.

Before you call, practice what you want to say ahead of time. You have to get your sales pitch just right and it's can't be too long. You really need to make your initial pitch in thirty-seconds or less. You don't want the reporter or editor to lose interest. He or she might be busy and facing a deadline. So, jot down some notes on what you want to say and practice your message a few times before making your call. Just make sure you don't sound like you are reading from a "script."

As you are preparing to make your call it's important that you remember to be patient. You might have to fight your way through a voice mail tree or you might get transferred to several of the "wrong people" until you reach the "right person". Don't get angry or snippy with the receptionist. Just tell them why you are calling and who you want to speak to. Be persistent, but also be friendly. You can't risk alienating anyone.

Once you've finally reached the "right person" explain who you are, what group you are with, why you are calling and why what information you are relaying is important. Remember to get to your point quickly. The reporter will appreciate that.

You can never predict how your cold call will turn out. The person you've reached might be very receptive, or very standoffish. Be prepared for anything. Also be prepared to get nothing but voice mail. If that happens just leave the message that you have written down and rehearsed. Make sure that you relay all the important information.

It's important to keep some kind of written record of whom you called and when you called them. Keep records of the media outlets, the people you reached, the date and the time that you made the call. By keeping good records you reduce the risk of calling the same places multiple times – that can be annoying for those that you call. A written record can also serve as a reminder of media outlets that require follow up calls.

As I mentioned earlier, be persistent but don't be a pest. If you are too aggressive and too pesky you will earn the reputation of being a pain in the neck and you won't be taken seriously in the future.

Here's one more piece of advice regarding cold calls: don't make them in-person. Whatever you do DO NOT drop by a television station, a radio station or a newspaper unannounced. Trust me. Reporters and editors find it annoying and disruptive. They also might end up thinking that are a little off your rocker.

When I was a reporter in Sacramento I got a call in the

newsroom from the front desk saying that there was a guy out front who insisted on talking with a reporter. He wasn't going to leave unless he did. I answered the phone at the wrong time, just my luck. I went into the lobby and met with a crazed looking individual carrying stacks and stacks of papers. He insisted that the papers he carried served as proof of several great government conspiracies and he wanted to share them with a reporter and have his story told. After spending a few minutes with the gentleman, his story began to unfold but that story seemed to be more about doses of medication he neglected to take rather than government cover-ups.

Eventually, I showed our visitor the door. His story never made the news. And I never met with an unexpected guest to a newsroom again.

The Pitch Letter or E-mail

One way to get your foot in the media door...

One good way to begin making media contacts is through sending a letter, or e-mail, of introduction to assignment editors, reporters and writers telling them about you and your group. It will arrive to the members of the media out of the blue, but it will be a good foot in the door.

Include with this letter any other materials about your group or organization that you'd like to send: pamphlets, brochures, fact sheets and maybe even some brief bios of your group leaders. However, it is important to remember that you should **NOT** send them a ton of stuff because a lot of the materials will be discarded. Just send the basic materials with your initial introduction.

Here's is a sample initial pitch message:

DATE
NAME
TITLE
MEDIA OUTLET
ADDRESS
CITY, STATE ZIP

Dear SALUTATION:

I recently came across your article in LOCAL PUBLICATION which touched on (YOUR AREA OF EXPERTISE). I would like to introduce you to NAME OF YOUR ORGANIZATION/GROUP and let you know how we can provide you with credible sources for future news stories in our area of concentration.

Let me give you a little background on us: INCLUDE A BRIEF DESCRIPTION OF YOUR GROUP/ORGANIZATION AND WHAT YOU DO. INCLUDE THE NUMBER OF MEMBERS THAT YOU HAVE AND INCLUDE SOME IMPRESSIVE PARTNERSHIPS IF YOU HAVE THEM.

I am confident that members of our company/ group/ organization would be excellent resources for future stories.

In the meantime, I've included copies of a few past articles on us which I hope you will find to be helpful.

If you would like to set up an interview for any of your future stories I would be happy to connect you with an expert within our organization/group/company.

Thank you for your time and please keep us in mind for any future questions that you may have regarding YOUR AREA OF EXPERTISE.

Sincerely,

NAME
JOB TITLE

If you are sending a hard copy letter, don't forget to also include a few business cards. While the reporter might not keep the other materials you send, he or she will usually hang onto business cards and keep them in a stack near for phone for future use. Reporters always need good contacts. You could become one of them. However, remember that whether you are shooting off an e-mail or an actual letter, there is a good chance the message might go unanswered. But it is a risk worth taking!

Start Drafting a General Pitch Letter that You Can Use to Introduce Yourself to the Media

Thing 16

Event Planning

You have a lot of planning to do…

If you are putting together some kind of event, like a press conference, a park dedication, a ribbon-cutting ceremony or an announcement regarding the receipt of a large grant, then you have a lot of planning ahead of you. There are many, many things to do.

The following is an event planning checklist that you might find helpful:

Things to do BEFORE your event

Determine the event's goals. Figure out what it is that you hope your event will accomplish. It will help you decide the appropriate event to hold. Also, mapping out your objectives will help you evaluate the level of your success after the event is over.

Create a planning committee. Put together a group of people and assign them the task of organizing the event. Form a committee and have members develop a system of checks and balances and divide duties. Also have members create a timeline and assign tasks.

Determine audience and scope of the event. Ask yourself some serious logistical questions: Why are you holding this event? Who will you invite? Is this a small, medium or large event? Internal or external? Will you be inviting attendees to tour your facility? Will this event take place before, during or after regular business hours?

Select date and time. Carefully look over your calendar so that you can coordinate with all of the key speakers, participants, and guest/s of honor you are planning to have participate in your event. Make sure the event doesn't conflict with other big community events in your area which might attract the people you want to attract.

Find a location and check availability. Time for some more questions: What location will best serve your event? Will this be a formal or casual setting? Will it be held indoors or outside? If you want to hold it outdoors, what will you do in the event of bad weather? Do you need special permits for any outdoor gatherings?

Put together a project budget. How much is this going to cost you and who will be paying for it all? Don't forget all associated costs such as catering, printing, mailing, rentals, gratuities, tax, and any outside services.

Decide on printed materials. Are you going to print out invitations, programs, flyers or related publications? If so, what do you want them to look like?

Alerting the media. Media advisories and press releases need to go out well before the scheduled events. Make sure this is included in your timeline.

Photography. Think about hiring a professional photographer to document your event. The pictures can be used for internal publications, newsletters, Web sites, lobby decorations, or even as gifts to present to attending dignitaries at a later date. If you don't have the money to hire a pro then maybe you or someone on your staff can snap a few pictures with a good quality digital camera.

Things to do the DAY OF your event

Get there early. You will have to make sure that volunteers and other helpers are there and ready to work. Make sure all of your supplies are in place: food, beverages, equipment, tables, chairs, etc. Make sure everything is set up and ready to go.

Review the day's agenda. Prioritize projects and make any necessary adjustments. Make sure everyone knows who to ask if they have questions. Assign more tasks, if needed.

Monitor the event's progress. Make sure things are going smoothly and move staff and volunteers around if necessary.

Do a debriefing. After the event, don't forget to thank the staff and volunteers who helped you. Go over any unfinished event-related jobs and ask everyone for input on what went right, what went wrong and what could be done to make things go more smoothly in the future.

Things to do AFTER your event

Get those thank-you letters in the mail. People like to be thanked for their efforts. Make sure you properly thank your staff, volunteers and also any guest speakers who helped you. Let them know that you appreciate their help and that their involvement made a difference to your event.

Spread the word. If you have an internal newsletter, or one that you send out to clients or members, this would be the perfect time to write an article about your event and trumpet your success. Use a lot of photographs.

Evaluate everything that you have done associated with your event to determine if you met – or exceeded – your original objectives.

Rest and plan for the next event! You can't stop now. You are on a roll!

Thing 17

Learn How to Get the RIGHT PEOPLE Together

Community Forums

A good way to get people together to spread your message...

If you are the operator of a nonprofit organization or a community-based group it's important for you to know that one of the best ways to reach out to the public is through staging community forums. These gatherings have the potential of bringing together people in your community to hear your message, and there is always the possibility that your forums might attract media coverage. So, these forums can serve more than one purpose.

Community forums are a good opportunity for people to gather your stakeholders in one place and speak with one voice about a certain topic or issue. While there is always room for discussion at these gatherings, they should not be confused with debates where groups with opposing viewpoints face off and challenge each other's stances on certain issues. You want to organize community forums to have people unite behind your cause, whatever your cause may be.

Staging community forums can be a lot of work. However, even if you have a very small staff, by following these suggested steps you should be able to hold a successful community forum and bring people together to hear your message.

The following steps to staging community forums are simple:

Develop Your Topic:

This might seem like a given but it is important that you determine exactly what the topic of your forum is and what you are hoping to get out of your group discussion. You are probably saying "Yeah, no duh." However, you have to make sure that all parties invited are on the same page and are fully aware of what everyone will be talking about when they all get in the same room.

When you are contacting people to invite them to your forum, whether they are serving as panel members, guests or audience members, make it perfectly clear to them what everyone will be talking about and the purpose for your event. Explain that it will <u>not</u> be an all-purpose complaint session, but that your forum has a specific focus, whatever the focus may be.

For example, let's say you lead a community group that is concerned about the heavy traffic around your area school. You want to hold a community forum to get enough people together to show city planners that many people are concerned about the safety of the children and the staff at that school. Your obvious topic is "traffic safety around the school." Your goal is to get speed bumps, more stop signs, and better enforcement around the campus. Somewhere in your planning you might contact someone that you think could serve as a good forum panelist. However, after spending five minutes on the phone with this person you learn that his main gripe is new home construction and the traffic it creates. He wants to talk about a moratorium on new home building. While his concern might be a valid one, it is not the main concern that you share. That means he's not the right kind of panelist for the forum you are planning. He might have a good message, but it is NOT your message.

Determine Your Audience:

Figure out who your audience is, or if there are several audiences that you are trying to reach. It's important to zero in on your audience so that you can better narrow your focus. When in the planning stages of any community forum, there are several target audiences to consider: neighbors, parents, teachers, school district officials, local government and community leaders, and local business owners. Many times their concerns and interests overlap. Remember that when you are developing your messages you are aiming at the previously mentioned groups. These are the people that you are trying to bring together so that they will all work together.

For example, if you are trying to gather support to build new baseball fields in your local communities you want to make sure you are reaching out to families with children and to sports organizations. You'd be wasting your time trying to connect with senior citizens groups or organizations that get together and admire each other's classic cars that are built from kits. Know your targets well.

Select Your Panel and Moderator:

Selecting your panel is very important because it will take on the responsibility of sending your message out to the local community. You have to make certain that each panel member – while providing his or her own subject matter expertise – must also be on target with the message that you are trying to project. You all have to be talking about the same things otherwise you risking sending out multiple or muddy messages.

While it is important for your panel to get input from members of the public who might have very differing points of view, it is very important that your group of hand-selected speakers agree in principle with the message that you are trying to convey. You DO NOT want to create a debate among your panelists because your general public audience could end up being confused and not receive the message that you want to send.

Make sure that your panelists all have knowledge about the subject, and that they perform different kinds of jobs in that subject area. This will prove their legitimacy to those in attendance.

Select a moderator who is a good public speaker with the skills to move the panelists along while still allowing them to have the time to make their points. Your moderator should have basic working knowledge of the subject without feeling the need to serve as another panelist.

It is also a good idea to invite a member of the local media to serve as a moderator, if possible. This serves several purposes: it helps educate more members of the press about your specific topic, it increases the chances that your issue will get some media coverage by tapping a local media person as your moderator, and having someone who is "well known" serve as moderator might help create more interest from the community.

During community forums there is always the possibility that people in the audience will try to turn the meeting into a debate, or some form of the Jerry Springer Show. Be respectful if they are asking questions or speaking out of turn and politely remind them that all panelists will remain after the formal discussion is over to speak with people individually if they'd like. This is a polite way of saying "Please don't shout out questions. We'll talk with you later."

Select Your Topic Questions:

It is important that you develop a list of discussion questions in advance. While all of your panelists know why they are participating in your forum, it's imperative that they not be taken by surprise with any of the questions being asked. You want them to be as well-prepared as possible. Give your panel members at least one-week's lead time to look over the questions and prepare their answers.

Make sure as you formulate your questions that they are designed to keep your panelists on task. While you are encouraging a healthy and lively discussion you don't want them to stray too far from the topic or the message.

Since your panelists will have expertise in different areas of the same topic, make sure that your moderator directs specific questions to those panelists, and also allows for feedback or response from other panel members.

Publicizing Your Forum:

Okay, so you've gone to all the trouble to line up the people you want speaking at your forum. Now, how do you publicize it so that people will actually come and participate? You have several plans of action here. First, since you have already established your target audience, go through that audience to help "spread the word."

For example, let's say your target audience is parents with young children. How would you publicize your event to that group? There are several avenues to pursue: local schools, PTAs, church or community groups, sports organizations, and day care centers. The list could be endless. Create a flyer detailing the date, time, location and purpose of your forum and start passing them out to the members of these groups. Ask them to post the flyers in places they feel their group members will see them.

Another great way of publicizing your forum is through contact with your local newspaper. When you call the paper ask to speak with an editor and tell that person who you are and what your forum is about. Tell that editor the importance of your event and who will participate. Ask if the editor believes this information is worthy of news coverage, or at the very least, a mention in the calendar of events portion of the paper.

Also consider contacting your local televisions stations and ask to speak with someone in their public service department. Many television stations also make "community calendar" announcements on the air and on their Web sites. With enough advance notice your forum could be placed on such a calendar.

After you are finished speaking with the public service department asked to be transferred to the news department's assignment desk and talk to an editor there. Explain the purpose of your call. Tell the editor about your upcoming forum and it's possible that you could generate some general news interest. It's worth a try!

Enter and Sign in Please:

Just before your event starts, as people are beginning to pile into your venue, direct them to the sign-in sheets you will place near the entrance. Explain that you are looking for others to help with your cause and that you are searching for new, enthusiastic members. However, also tell them that they should **only** sign-in if they are interested in getting more information from you.

When you ask attendees to enter and sign in, please, ask them to provide the following information: name, address, phone number and e-mail address. This data will prove to be useful to you later, after the event is over, after the chairs are stacked, the lights are out and you are still working for your cause.

The e-mail addresses will come in very handy when you start sending out your news releases to interested parties. However, it is always good to ask first if the folks are okay with being added to your list.

Your Forum Format:

The format of your forum can take on many different shapes and styles but the one thing you want to make sure of is that your discussion is well organized and orderly. While you want to encourage some debate you don't want to have your panel discussion start to resemble a day-time television talk show. You want to maintain order.

Here is a tried and true community forum format that works well:

Welcoming remarks: This is the beginning of the program where certain people welcome the panel and audience members. Those who customarily are invited to give welcoming remarks include hosts, school officials, organization leaders, local dignitaries such as elected officials and school board members.

Introductions and Ground Rules: This is the point where your moderator will introduce your panelists to the audience. It is important that your moderator have the exact name and title of each panel member so that they can be properly introduced. At this time, it is appropriate for your moderator to explain the forum ground rules to the audience, telling how things will be run. If you tell people early enough what to expect they will likely settle in, participate and enjoy the show.

Opening Remarks from Panelists: Allow your panelists the opportunity to each take a few minutes for self-introduction and to give his/her explanation of expertise. Please tell them to be brief and not talk for more than a few minutes. You don't want your audience to get bored before your forum really starts to cook. Each panelist can even offer a few opinions on the topic of discussion. This portion of the program lets the audience members learn who is who.

Begin Your Discussion: Start with your first pre-prepared question for one of your panelists. After that panelist has answered, allow each of the other panel members the opportunity to respond or provide additional information before moving on to the next question. Allow some room for discussion between the moderator and the panelists, but you DO NOT want your panelists to start debating each other. Also, tell your panelists to limit their answers to a minute or so. You want things to move quickly and you want your audience to lose interest.

Audience Questions: Allow for enough time at the end – around fifteen minutes or so - to give members of your audience the opportunity to ask questions. This brings the community into the discussion and this is what you want. You want their input and their opinions. You want to hear about their wants and needs.

It works best if you provide index cards to the audience at the beginning of the forum and ask them to write down their questions in advance. At some point during the forum have a member of your staff collect the index cards and start compiling questions for your panelists. If, by chance, you exhaust all of your hand-written, submitted questions this is the time to have your moderator ask if anyone in the audience has a questions they would like to ask.

Closing Remarks: Just as you did with your opening remarks, you should also give your panel members the chance to offer closing, summary remarks. This helps bring closure to the event. This also gives panelists an opportunity to invite members of the audience to approach them with individual questions at the close of the program. Closing remarks also give panelists the opportunity to provide the public with contact information they'd like to publicize: phone numbers, addresses, e-mail addresses or Web site addresses.

Thank Yous: This is where the moderator thanks each panel member for participating in the discussion and offers any closing remarks of his/her own.

There are several other things to consider when organizing a community forum. These are just some of the things to keep in mind. There are always others you could add to this list:

- Will your audience consist of only members of the general public who happen to hear about your forum by reading about it in the paper or seeing a flyer on a wall? Or do you also want to include invited guests as well? By including invited guests you increase the odds of having a larger, better informed audience.

- Make sure the place where you are holding your forum is large enough to handle a good-sized crowd, but the room shouldn't be so large that the crowd seems lost in the room. Sometimes it is hard to estimate how large your audience will be, but it's often better to have more people than room to make your forum looks well attended. At the same time, you don't want people sitting on the floor or in the aisles. Just use your best guess.

- Make sure that you have some kind of good, dependable sound system available with multiple microphones. You want your moderator to have his/her own microphone. It's okay if you have no more than two panelists sharing a microphone, but your goal is to keep it at two panelists only per microphone. You don't want your speakers to waste time passing a microphone between them. It slows down the program, stifles spontaneity and makes your event seem like you're doing it "on the cheap".

- If your organization or organizations with which your panelists are associated have any printed materials that can be distributed place them out on a table in the back of the room or near the refreshments (See next bullet point). Items such as flyers, brochures, and fact sheets are appropriate. When people attend events such as these they like to take things home.

- No matter what time of day you schedule your forum make sure that you provide a variety of light snacks and drinks for the people who will be attending. Snacks can keep people happy.

- Consider creating a questionnaire or some type of evaluation form. This will help you get feedback on your event from the attendees.

What to Do When the Forum Ends:

So, you've gone through all the heavy lifting of staging a community forum. You've brought all these people together to learn about your cause. What do you do now? Remember all those names, numbers and addresses you collected earlier? Contact those people and try to enlist their help in your cause. That's one of the reasons you brought them all together in the first place. Good luck!

So, now that you have all of this work done so far, do you know who to contact at the media outlets? If you don't, then read on. You'll find out.

Your Forum Planning Checklist

Make Sure You Pay Close Attention to Detail

- ✓ What's your chosen topic?

- ✓ Who is your audience?

- ✓ Who do you want serving as your panelists and moderator?

✓ What are your topic questions?

✓ What's the best way for you to publicize your event?

✓ Did you remember your sign-in sheet for the back of the room?

✓ How will you follow up with your audience members and the press?

Thing 18

Learn How Local NEWSROOMS Work

The Newspaper Newsroom

Who do you contact to pitch your story or make contact?

Let's talk about making contact with the newspaper newsroom. Where do you start, and whom do you contact if you are trying to pitch a news story?

First, take this little quiz and test your knowledge:

Let's say that you have a great story to tell about how your neighborhood association is cleaning up a nasty vacant lot where law breakers dump trash and sometimes gather to do what law breakers do. As association president you are planning a huge, one-day event where people from the local community are getting together to clean things up. You are expecting local dignitaries such as elected officials, sports figures and other community leaders to pitch in and join the fun. So, where do you begin initiating contact?

Do you start with (A) the reporter whose byline you read every day?

What about (B) a columnist? You might not always agree with what he or she writes but you think your story might be worth a mention in an upcoming column.

How about contacting (C) the editor who pores over and corrects the copy of the reporter and the columnist?

Or, what about (D) the BIG BOSS who has so much money that he owns the local TV station and the newspaper in your hometown?

Actually, newspapers seem to have several options: either A, B or C, the reporter, the editor or the columnist will work.

Newspapers have more in-roads than television or radio stations. Learn how to use them.

If you are planning on contacting an individual reporter first then the best way to find the best contact is by doing your homework. Read the local paper, or papers, to determine if there are certain reporters who seem to write about these types of issues: community stories, social issues, feature articles. If you find that one reporter's name is fixed with these types of stories more than any other then you have found your first point of contact. Initiate contact through a phone call, or an e-mail. Most newspapers not only list a reporter's byline (or name) with the story but those papers also often list contact information such as phone numbers and e-mail addresses.

If you get to speak with the reporter explain who you are and why you are calling. Tell the reporter you expect a lot of community involvement in your event. Tell the reporter you identified a problem in your community and that you have come up with a solution. All of these notions will help catch the reporter's attention.

You can use the same approach in contacting either the editor or the columnist. If you plan on contacting a columnist, again, do your homework. Make sure that the columnist you are contacting writes about these types of issues. For example, you would not want to consider contacting your paper's political columnist about your neighborhood clean-up event. You are better off tracking down a columnist who concentrates on social issues. Newspapers have several columnists on staff, so you should have several from which to choose.

It's also a good idea to start building relationships with individual newspaper editors as well. These folks are high level decision makers and are very influential in determining how stories are covered and what elements should be included.

Don't be discouraged if when you call these folks that they don't spend a great deal of time with you on the phone. These are busy people, but they will appreciate you making contact with them, if not for the story you called them about, but at least for future stories.

Remember, when you are making these contacts that you will be planting very important seeds!

The TV Newsroom

Who do you contact to pitch your story or make contact?

Let's talk about making media contacts with television news operations if you have a story to pitch. Let's use the same scenario we talked about in the previous chapter: the big neighborhood clean-up event.

Where do you start when making a story pitch to a television news station?

Do you start with (A) the highly popular anchor who hasn't covered a story in about 15 years? I mean, why not? You've watched this person on TV for years and feel as if you already know him or her very well. After all, that anchor is always in your living room delivering the news!

Or what about (B) the news producer who works on putting news programs together on a daily basis? You don't know who the producer is by name, but the name's not hard to find out. You just call the main number and ask for the producer of an individual newscast or program.

Do you (C) make a call to the BIG BOSS who runs the place but probably has never met a single member of the news team? I mean, you've read about this guy in the local paper. He's got a lot of money and seems influential, and he owns a TV station!

Or do you (D) contact the reporter that you watch on your local news every night, who you see covering everything from fires to birthday parties for 100 year old snowboarders? Again, this is another person you've "invited into your home" for several years. Why not pitch a story idea to someone who actually goes out and covers news stories for a living?

There are two answers: either B or D, the producer or the reporter.

Producers are good points of contact because they bear the responsibility of determining the direction of their newscasts. They decide what stories will run and where they will run within the body of their news program. Bear in mind that there are several kinds of producers working at television stations. There are individual newscast producers who put together the 5:00 p.m. or 11:00 p.m. news programs, or there are producers who create segments such as health and fitness or education. It's possible that the show producer you contact might direct you to a segment producer who specializes in certain areas. That's a good thing because these folks are always searching for story ideas and most likely, they at least will listen to what you have to say.

Contacting individual reporters is also an excellent option. These folks also are always searching for story ideas to pitch to their bosses. Initiate contact with a brief phone call or a brief e-mail. If you provide too much information at the outset then you risk alienating that reporter right away. Initially, just offer the basic facts and see if the reporter shows some interest. Offer to introduce the reporter to more people to interview. Make yourself a helpful resource.

One potential television newsroom contact that we did not include in our quiz is someone known as the assignment editor. This is the person who helps oversee a television station's news coverage by assigning reporters and photographers, scheduling interviews, booking satellite feeds and acting like a general air traffic controller. An initial call to an assignment editor can also serve as a good foot in the door at television news stations. These are the folks who can direct you to the right people if they can't help you at the time that you are calling.

Always remember: please don't get discouraged if the people you call in the television newsroom don't spend much time with you on the phone. Television newsrooms – just like newspaper newsrooms – are very busy places. Don't take it personally if the person you contact just asks for a name and phone number where you can be reached and then hangs up. Many times journalists don't have much spare time. If you do get their attention, just use that time wisely. It will pay off in the long run.

Types of media outlets
All media is NOT alike...

Media comes in many forms. Some connect with more people than others but all forms of media are effective. It is possible to make contact with the decision makers involved with all these types of media outlets, but that will take an investment of time and energy on your part to track down the right people.

Electronic
- Television—regular, cable and community access
- Radio—public, all news, news/talk, music format
- Computer—Web pages 'zines, e-mail, user groups

Print
- Newspapers
- Magazines
- Newsletters

Other
- Community bulletin boards

- Billboards
- Direct mail
- Electronic signage

Make phone calls, use the Web, however you decide to start tracking down people to put in your "media contact list", start doing that soon and keep the file organized and up-to-date.

Thing 19

Learn How to Deal with REPORTERS

If a reporter calls

What do you do? How do you handle it?

Sometimes reporters just show up at your door. Sometimes they call out of the blue. If either situation occurs, what do you do? Will you know how to handle things? Here is a quick list of things to remember:

Don't Panic: Take a deep breath. Wait for the reporter to explain why you are being contacted. Reporters don't just call when times are bad. Remember to ask how you can help.

Ask about the nature of the story: One of the first things you want to ask is "what is your story about?" Once you find that out, either ask the reporter to wait outside your office or offer to call the reporter back so that you can take a few minutes to collect your thoughts or gather information. At that point, try and determine how your participation in the story might help you with your media relations goals. Once you've determined that you can start figuring out how you will be responding.

Gather Your Thoughts: Think! Don't answer a question without first thinking about the answer. Off the cuff answers are not always the best. Since you are now <u>not</u> panicking and have taken a moment to ask the reporter what the story is about, you have bought yourself some time to formulate your answers. In most cases, you probably don't have to answer right away. It's okay to say, "Let me call you right back." Once you've said that you can reflect on how you will respond.

It's really important that you take the time and put some thought into your responses. If you don't state your answer clearly, or give the answer you'd really like to give, the reporter may not understand what you meant to say. You want to provide thoughtful answers in order to portray yourself in the best possible light.

Never Say Anything Is "Off the Record": While you might have the urge to gain the reporter's confidence by saying something "off the record" it's best not to say anything you don't want to be reported. While you can generally trust a reporter by asking if you can go "off the record" it's really not something you want to do. Most reporters will respect your request, but they are required to attribute their information to sources and will likely be pressed by their bosses to do so. Assume anything you say will be quoted.

Respond: Reporter have tough deadlines. Respect those deadlines. If a reporter has taken the time to contact you and request your participation in a story then the very least you can do is call that reporter back in a timely fashion, whether or not you decide to participate.

What does "timely fashion" mean? That depends. If you speak with a reporter one of the final questions you should ask before hanging up and deciding what to do is "what's your deadline?" Most likely, the reporter will say "today" or "within a couple of hours". That means you should respond quickly, such as in an hour or less. The reporter needs to know if he can count on you or not. If you are able to participate in the story, great! Call that reporter back right away. If you cannot or would rather not be involved call that reporter back right away any way and let him know. If there's one thing that makes a reporter angry it is when a potential interview subject fails to call back with either a "yes" or "no" answer. Don't leave a reporter hanging. Call back.

Thank The Reporter: Be polite. Why? Well, because that's the way your mother raised you. Even if the reporter might be pushy, or seem disorganized, or seem to act like a mean person you must still be polite just as you would with a potential customer or a constituent. Consider it another form of customer service.

After the story has run on the news – and this also applies to stories that appear in print – take the time to send that reporter a thank you note, or even place a quick call. Thank the reporter for his/her time and follow up with an invitation to call you back for future stories.

If the reporter made a mistake in his story then take a moment to politely point out the error, but don't come off as angry or combative. You don't want to create any enemies. If it is a serious error then it is appropriate that you ask for a retraction or a clarification to be made. But, again, only ask for a retraction or a clarification if the mistake made is serious enough to cause problems.

If the reporter got the story right for the most part and didn't make any critical gaffes, then let the petty errors slide and be pleased that you got some coverage.

What reporters like

A simple list of helpful things...

News reporters, assignment editors, writers and other media decision makers don't have much time during their average work day, so they don't like it when people waste their time.

Media representatives like, respect and continue working with business owners, and organization leaders who:

- Are honest
- Understand how the media works and are accommodating to deadlines
- Give reporters sufficient lead time
- Have spokespeople and other representatives lined up, informed and ready to talk when the reporter arrives
- Are aware of the information the reporter is seeking and

not try to deceptively steer them in another direction
- Are willing to be helpful to make a story work
- Offer news crews something to drink (water, soft drinks, ice tea, NEVER alcohol!)
- Offer help in carrying heavy equipment (They'll likely decline this offer because their equipment is expensive and their responsibility, but it's polite to offer!)
- Don't get offended when stories don't run
- Point out in polite and tactful ways when the reporter and his/her story is inaccurate
- Are appreciative of the reporter's efforts and send a personal "thank you" card or letter, or even a letter of appreciation to his/her boss

It's a simple list, but if you follow it closely you will be able to develop solid relationships with reporters and media executives who will look upon you as a credible source, and one to call upon when needed.

What reporters DO NOT like

A simple list of non-helpful things...

As stated on the previous page, news reporters, assignment editors, writers and other media decision makers don't have much time during their average work day, so they don't like it when people waste their time. We can't emphasize that enough.

The following is a list of things that you **SHOULD NOT DO** if you want to have success in dealing with the media:

- Don't lead them on by promising one story but trying to get them to do another
- Don't threaten to go "over their heads" if they are not interested in your story
- Don't send them gifts to convince them to cover your story. In some circles, these are also called "bribes."
- Don't send them twenty page faxes and one-inch thick

media kits because those will only be tossed out and not read
- Don't leave them really, really, really long and rambling voice-mail messages that go on and on and on and on
- Don't waste their time while they are visiting you by giving them all kinds of information about your last fishing trip, son's soccer game or anything that has nothing to do with their story
- Don't ramble on while you are being interviewed because the reporter will stop listening to you at some point
- Don't suddenly assume the reporter is your new best friend and wants to hang out with you or come over for dinner
- Don't pester the reporter (specifically the television or radio reporter) about sending you copies of the story because they will likely never call upon you again

The list of things NOT to do is longer than the list of things TO DO. Use these lists together to improve your chances of success in dealing with the media.

Thing 20

Understand the Basics of the PRESS CONFERENCE

Press Conferences

When and how to stage them...What to say...

When should you hold press conferences? The answer: When you have something fairly important to say or announce.

- If you have a big event like a grand opening, a major task force meeting, a large grant being awarded from some really rich foundation, let the press know. There's never a guarantee of coverage but there's always the chance.
- You can hold a press conference when there's some new research or new developments in an on-going program to unveil. If you have a new partnership you are proud of, or an innovative product to introduce, it might make for a good story.
- You can also hold press conferences if you have answers to community concerns such as a rash of break-ins, or efforts to raise money to build a new community park.

Whatever reason you have to hold a press conference—and it has to be an honest, legitimate reason—here are a few simple things to keep in mind when setting the process in motion:

- Have three to five speakers ready. Any more speakers from the podium and you will lose your audience.
- Make people accessible after the press conference for individual interviews. Open with brief statements first and then take questions later. This will give you a chance to state your case before the questions start flying at you. Look for positive angles. Take the high road. Speak about your organization and what you are doing.

- Recognize the naysayers but don't stoop to their level. Use a podium and have a logo displayed. This provides instant recognition. It's like "product placement" in the movies.
- If your event is away from the office, tell your office staff all the details to accommodate reporters who are running late.

Thing 21

Prepare YOURSELF to Talk... and Prepare Some More

The Interview

It's time for the interview. How can you prepare?

Do <u>your</u> homework! Learn about the reporter, the program, the media outlet, the column. Does this person seem to have a tendency to take a negative approach to things? Does he seem to give people a fair shot?

Before you even answer one question take the time to **ask the reporter what the story is about.** In most cases, the first approach from the press is over the phone. Ask the reporter "what kinds of questions will you be asking?" "What areas will be covered?" You have the right to know these things.

Anticipate the reporter's needs and questions. Put yourself in the reporter's place and **think about what questions you would ask** of someone in your position. And while you are preparing for your interview try to anticipate the questions that you'd **least like to be asked** and come up with some answers.

Keep in mind that reporters will ask lots of follow up questions. Despite what you might see in some Hollywood movie, **reporters are not dedicated to trying to "trip you up."** At least most of them don't operate that way. Most of them are looking for consistency in your answers. Try to stay on your intended path.

Most important: **develop message points**. You don't have to carry them with you but work on them. Write them out. Think of four or five key points that you want to emphasize and keep trying to come back to them. Remember them.

And another thing: **practice your answers**. Repeat your answers and message points over and over. If you are driving to the interview, rehearse your answers in the car. Wear the hand-free device to your cell phone so that at least you can feel like you are talking to someone, and so the folks in the other cars won't think you are just talking to yourself.

Thing 22

Never say "NO COMMENT"
... never... ever

The Danger of saying "No Comment"

Why saying "no comment" is no good...

You've seen this scenario countless times on the evening news (or in the movies): someone is attempting to force his way through a gauntlet of reporters while entering a courtroom, or leaving an office building. The salivating and story-hungry reporters are relentlessly firing question after question at the person.

"What about those charges against you?"

"What do you have to say about this investigation?"

"How do you answer those allegations made in the paper this morning?"

You can insert whatever questions you want. The point is that we have set the scene and you get the idea here. In this scenario reporters are asking questions and demanding answers. The person in question is getting hammered from all sides, and all the while, as he fights his way through the crowd he's shouting those two little words that just encourage reporters to keep asking questions. Those two little words: NO COMMENT.

To a reporter – and I used to be one, so I am not making this up and speak from experience – answering questions with the phrase "no comment" is an open invitation for reporters to keep asking questions until they get some kind of answer. Reporters are not trying to be rude, in most cases, but they are expected to come back to their offices with some kind of interview, some kind of quote, for their stories. While the potential interview subject might have been instructed by an attorney to refrain from answering, or the person is so scared that he doesn't know what to say, an answer of "no comment" is simply no good.

Now, any lawyers out there who are reading this are probably shaking their heads and thinking that the guy writing this book doesn't know what he's talking about. If a person is told by an attorney or a boss or some superior officer not to comment, then how can this be disputed?

What I am saying is that it's okay NOT to offer a detailed comment, but it's NOT okay to say "no comment." It really doesn't do you any good. However, what's important to understand is that there are ways to not comment while you are commenting. Confused? What I mean is that there are ways of answering questions without saying too much, or saying much of anything.

Here are some examples:

Let's say that you are the operator of a well-known nonprofit organization that has a name synonymous with everything that is good in your local community. Your group hands out awards to local scouts and has a scholarship fund for underprivileged high school kids who want to go to college. Everyone in the community loves and respects your group. However, one day it's learned that an employee of yours is taking donated goods from the storage room and selling them at flea markets and pocketing the cash. You are not implicated at all, but you are asked by investigators to come in and answer a few questions in order to help them figure things out. As you leave the police headquarters, the sidewalk outside is lined with reporters and cameras. There is no back exit to use. You have to walk past the media, and as you do, reporters are firing questions at you. Keep in mind, the case is under investigation and your attorney has warned you not to say anything to the press. What do you do?

You have a few options; you could walk past without saying a word. You could keep repeating "No comment. No comment." Or you could stop and answer a few questions. Again, keep in mind that you can provide answers to the press without unveiling a great deal of information, or getting yourself in trouble.

You can say something like: "Ladies and gentlemen, our attorneys are advising us as this time not to talk about the case. It's under investigation and we're not going to say anything. However, let me say that we will fully cooperate with the investigation and help in any way that we can. We are sorry for what's happening right now. Like you, we also want answers to these questions so that we can assure that the public still has confidence in our organization."

Then you move on.

And there you go. You provided an answer for the press without giving up any information that could get you in trouble, or get your lawyer really, really mad at you. The reporters might not have the quote they were hoping for, but they did get a quote nonetheless. You didn't run. You didn't hide. You stood there and said something. What you have done by handling the situation in this way is present yourself in the most positive light possible. By not running and by not hiding you have presented yourself as a "stand up" person. You look trustworthy and believable.

You might be wondering: why should I say anything at all? Why not just be totally silent or say "no comment" and brush past the reporters with their tape recorders and microphones waving in my face. Well, the answer is simple. It might seem unfair, but it's simple. Many people might interpret your complete silence or your terse "no comment" to actually mean "I have something to hide and I am certainly not going to say anything for the evening news!" While people should not assume that a "no comment" statement equates with guilt, unfortunately many people still feel that way. When it plays out that way on the TV news or in the paper that way then it doesn't reflect well on you.

If and when you find yourself stuck in these types of situations, or you anticipate this happening, start thinking of ways to say something without saying anything that will only make matters worse. Providing those kinds of answers takes preparation and planning, but it's possible.

Keep in mind that by doing this that you are not trying to be evasive. You are not trying to outwit the reporters because that rarely works in the end. You just can't answer the questions being asked of you. However you really should try to say something because you want the media representatives to have some form of **your** side of the story as they are putting their stories together for publication. You might not be giving them the definitive answer they are seeking, but at least you are giving them something.

Back in July of 2006, National Public Radio Reporter Martin Kaste found himself working on a story where his intended interview subject ended up having way too much revealed because that subject said way too little from the get-go.

The Pentagon had a public relations program underway at the time called "America Supports You." It was a feel-good campaign geared toward troops stationed in dangerous parts of the world overseas. The kind of "soft and fuzzy" kind of story that you'd think a government agency would be salivating to talk about.

However, when Kaste began asking questions the Pentagon was supplying no answers. They kept putting him off until at one point a Pentagon representative suggested that he submit questions in writing and answers would eventually follow. Any reporter would ask himself/herself: "Are you kidding? A feel-good program like this and I am being told to submit my questions in writing? There must me something wrong here!"

What happened was this: The stalling gave NPR's Kaste time to really dig. What he found was that "America Supports You" was costing the Pentagon more than $2.5 million in private public relations contracts for its first year. NPR also found a program related "teaching supplement" in **Weekly Reader** – that's a periodical aimed at third-graders. The program was reaching out to little kids with public relations information about the war.

The Pentagon's stalling and refusal to say something at the outset gave Kaste a lot of time to test the program's online "message to the troops" system. What the reporter found out was that those overseeing the "message to troops system", apparently edited out political content in the messages. The information that was allowed to remain: words of praise about President Bush, supportive information about soldiers finishing the job in Iraq, and words of criticisms geared toward people protesting the war.

We will never know for certain whether the Pentagon, by just saying a few nice words about the "America Supports You", would have been guaranteed a nice, positive and fluffy public relations piece on National Public Radio. However, by stalling, by not answering, by essentially saying "no comment", the Pentagon definitely did not get good PR mileage out of that story.

Thing 23

Remember that Things CAN Go Wrong

Managing the Media – and Yourself – During a Crisis

It's time to peer into the dictionary again. What's the definition of the word "crisis"?

- A turning point in the course of anything
- A decisive or crucial time
- A time of great danger or trouble, whose outcome decides whether possible bad consequences will follow

"Crisis" has many definitions of different lengths and detail. Basically, a crisis is any situation which requires immediate and coordinated action that could have significant impact on the organization or its reputation. A crisis is an unexpected event or series of events that create a lot of uncertainty that can threaten your organization's goals.

During a crisis, your group's reputation and image have to be managed just as any other organizational asset. The role of the mass media during crises has been a topic of discussion for a very long time. Criticism of how media handles itself dates back centuries. Thomas Jefferson once wrote: "The man who reads nothing at all is better educated than the man who reads nothing but newspapers." Many people still hold that type of mistrust today.

During times of crisis, there is a great deal of uncertainty and fear. People turn on their televisions, or log onto the Internet or check their Smartphone, to get the latest information, analysis of the current circumstances, and to make sense of things. Most people look to the media to reduce uncertainty and fear by receiving what they believe to be accurate information.

There are several questions that are raised about this. First, is the information sources are providing journalists accurate? Sometimes CEOs and spokespeople publicly react too quickly, without having all the facts, or the right facts. This can compound the crisis. Also, are the journalists accurately reporting the information? This cannot be guaranteed during crisis situations. It's up to professional communicators to monitor the reporting and speak up when inaccuracies are reported.

The news business today moves at lightning speed. Many stories now are broken on blogs or websites rather than in the Sunday morning newspaper or the 11:00 p.m. news. The race by news organizations to be the first and the fastest to report a big story means that now, more than ever before, it is vitally important that the news sources – CEOs, Board Presidents, and other executives – must learn how to react accurately, promptly and properly during crises.

Newspapers, news radio stations, 24-hour cable news operations and every other media outlet imaginable can have great impact, both negative and positive, on any given situation. A company cannot control how a news organization reports a story, but that organization can control how it interacts with a news organization and how it provides information.

During a crisis, an organization's future can hinge on how stakeholders perceive and react to how the company or organization handles a situation. Failing to communicate during a crisis is one of the biggest mistakes any organization can make.

By nature, humans don't really like to plan for crises. Basically, we don't want to plan for the possibility of bad things happening. However, the truth is that with acts of terrorism in our own country, with high profile incidents of workplace and school yard violence, it is important that you have some kind of plan in place no matter whether you are the owner of a medium-sized business or the operator of a small nonprofit organization.

The bottom line is that you need to learn how to deal with bad news.

Every business, every school, and every organization is required to have some kind of emergency evacuation plan in the event of some kind of crisis. For instance, companies practice fire drills. Employees know where to meet in the parking lot if the fire alarm goes off. But how many groups or organizations have a media crisis plan and practice it? The answer: very few. Most of your big city law enforcement agencies frequently stage disaster drills and part of those drills includes handling the media. But most organizations do not have a media crisis plan, or if they do have some kind of disaster drill down on paper that blueprint does not include how to deal with the media in the event of an emergency.

Think of a crisis media plan as being like an insurance plan; you don't really want to use it but when you do you are glad you have it. The difference between a media crisis plan and an insurance policy is that a plan will only cost you the time and effort it takes to put it together. You won't have to worry about rising premiums, that's for sure!

The best thing to do to prepare for a possible crisis is have a plan prepared and tucked away somewhere knowing that you will only pull it out of the drawer and blow the dust off it in case of emergencies. Think of a crisis media plan like the jack in the trunk of a car; you only pull it out and use it in the event of a flat tire. It's the same with a crisis media plan; you only use it on rare occasions.

So, how do you get started?

First, you need to realize that you have to make your plan simple and user-friendly. It can't be too long or complicated. Try to keep the rules to a minimum. Realize that you cannot anticipate every possible emergency that could hit. It's a waste of your time and the time of your staff members to try and craft crisis communications plans for every possible scenario you could face. Make your plan as general as possible so that you can adapt its use to various occasions.

Understand that the planning takes place long before there is any crisis. It is really difficult to craft any type of plan if you are creating one on the fly. It's like constructing a house without building plans – you never know what your end product is going to look like.

So, here we go with a helpful little checklist:

- Plan in advance for a crisis (which you are already doing, then good for you!)
- Put together a "crisis management" team that you can call into action quickly.
- Spell out what you want to accomplish
- Put your spokesperson into action (the one you should have already chosen)
- Develop key messages
- Determine the best channels of communications
- Stick with what you know.
- Be honest and open with reporters and avoid saying "no comment."
- Relax.
- Get professional communications help if necessary.

Here's a brief side note that's important to mention right now. Professional communications or public relations help might be **exactly what you need**. If that's the case, then seek the help. Just keep in mind that getting such help can be costly. Contracting with a professional communications firm can mean paying big bucks. If that firm assigns a junior executive to your account you can expect to pay at least $95 an hour to work on your project. An experienced account executive charges close to $150 an hour. BUT if they want to call in the big guns to handle your account – like a senior account executive – you can expect to be billed as much as $300 an hour. Check around but the rates are fairly standard in the communications business. Basically, talk AIN'T cheap!

Keep in mind that hiring an expensive professional communications firm, PR agency or communications specialist to work for you or your cause does not necessarily guarantee that you will get better results than if you hired a less expensive company to do the work. But the opposite isn't necessarily true either. But, as I've said before, if you think the job is too big for you then seek professional help.

Now, let's go over each one of these items briefly.

Plan in advance of a crisis: So, how does one do that? Obviously what we are saying is plan in the event a crisis occurs and not plan to have a crisis happen to you. The point is to be ready to react in case you have to. Have something written down in a binder and make sure that key members of your staff know that there is a plan that will need to be followed in the event of a crisis where the media is involved.

Meet with staff periodically to go over the plan so that everyone understands the proper protocol. You need to make sure that staff understands what steps your organization will take in the event that you have to enact your crisis media plan.

Put together a crisis management team that you can call into action quickly: Pick a handful of staff members that you know you can trust in moments of crisis to act responsibly. Assign separate tasks to them, some of them with the press, others might handle inquiries from the general public or constituents, others might deal with facilities issues, food and water, or even traffic control. Meet with your crisis management team periodically just to make sure that they are prepared in the event of an emergency.

Spell out what you want to accomplish: This means that you have to have a clear understanding of what you need to carry out during your "relationship under fire" with the media. Remind staff that your main objective is and always will be to be concerned for the safety and well-being of employees, that you must strive to portray your organization in the best light possible, and that you will always be honest and as open as possible during this time of crisis.

Put your spokesperson to work: We've already been over this, so hopefully you have hand-picked a person or two who will serve as the primary spokespeople to represent your company or organization. Inform everyone who answers a phone that if a call comes in from the media to direct any media inquiries to the spokesperson or spokespeople. Be firm in telling staffers that they are NOT TO ANSWER REPORTER'S QUESTIONS. You want to make sure that you are speaking with a united voice.

Your spokespeople could find themselves under a great deal of pressure, the kind they have never experienced before. So, make sure during times of crisis that they have no other duties to worry about so that they can concentrate on the crisis at hand. Give them space and give them support.

Develop key messages: Figure out what your spokespeople are going to say and how they are going to say it. Write it down and practice it. Stick to your message. Keep repeating the key points that you want to make and do your best to communicate with confidence.

We covered **key messages** earlier in this book. Key messages during a crisis are different compared to any other time of business, but the concept is essentially the same. Just think about what it is that you want to say publicly and say it. A word of caution here: there are times when there are some things that you just can't talk about for legal reasons. Maybe there's litigation involved or it's a sensitive legal matter. During these times, consider consulting your attorney – if you have one – to go over things that you cannot and should not say publicly.

Determine the best channels of communications: what's the best way to approach the dissemination of information? Start internally first. If some crisis is underway – and it's not immediately apparent to staff – let people within your organization know what's going on. Tell them the truth – or as much truth as you are able to unveil. You want to stamp out any potential rumors from the very beginning, otherwise there's no telling what kind of information could reach the public. The most important thing you can tell staff members is that all press inquires must go to the designated spokespeople. Consider calling an emergency staff meeting to let people know what's going on.

Now that you've dealt with internal matters it's time to look externally. How are you going to publicly respond? Will it be through a news release, a press conference, or by conducting individual interviews with reporters? If you are really getting hammered with interview requests, and the incident is an ongoing one, consider holding periodic news conferences so stay in touch with reporters and to make sure you can quash any rumors that begin to percolate.

The fastest way to communicate may be through your local news radio stations. If a crisis breaks involving your organization, consider contacting the news radio stations in your town and offering to have your spokespeople interviewed "live on the air" to tell the public what's happening.

Stick with what you know: If you are old enough you remember there once was an old police television drama called *Dragnet*. One of the main characters was the no-nonsense Sgt. Joe Friday and one of his favorite phrases when conducting interviews with victims and witnesses was "Just the facts, ma'am." Basically, what Joe was always trying to tell people was just tell what you know. Offer no speculation. Speculation can get you into hot water.

If a reporter is asking you about the circumstances surrounding a crisis tell that reporter only what you know. Do not hypothesize because that can lead to more conjecture and more rumors.

So, if you are ever questioned by a reporter pretend that person is the gruff Sgt. Friday and just stick to the facts, please.

Be honest and open with reporters and avoid saying "no comment": There's an entire section in this book dealing with the "no comment" issue. (You read it and remember everything, right?) Just let me say briefly here that saying "no comment" is the last thing you want to say to a reporter because it will only prompt that reporter to dig deeper or go elsewhere for facts. As you will read in that section, there are ways of answering questions without really answering. You are not trying to be evasive, but you are trying to make sure that you don't say the wrong thing at the wrong time.

Now, let's talk about the honesty issue. It is important that you be truthful with reporters at all times – or at least as truthful as you can possibly be – because lies and misconceptions have a nasty way of coming back to bite you. Once reporters have learned the real extent of the problem, and they realize you told them something completely different, they will automatically stop trusting you. They will even accuse you of trying to deceive them

Never, ever say anything to a reporter that you know is **not true.** If you do that you will lose your credibility **instantly.**

Relax: Can you believe that I'm telling you to relax? The nerve of me! It's easier said than done, but the truth is that you really need to calm down as much as possible during a crisis situation so that you can see things more clearly and think more clearly.

Breathe deeply. Lie down if you have to. Do whatever you have to do to calm yourself down because you know that panicking can only make matters worse.

Get professional communications help if necessary: There are some great communications companies out there who specialize in crisis management. If you have the means to contract with one to help you through a crisis involving the media, then do it. These folks are out there and they are ready to rock, if you need them.

Here is another list of things to remember when it comes to crisis communications planning:

- It's better to over-estimate the crisis than to under-estimate it. By over-estimating you will be able to use all the tools that you have in place to solve your problems quickly.
- When you are talking to the media about the crisis at hand remember the order of importance of your concerns: people always come first, property always second, and money is third. You know in your heart that's right any way, but it's important that you remember that sequence, otherwise you could be labeled as cold and callous.
- If the crisis was somehow preventable, you have to prepare a response to the question **"how can you prevent this from happening again?"** In fact, when you are crafting your message points, that's something to include. Make sure that your answers are also "solution oriented." Have your solutions ready.
- Monitor the coverage in progress for accuracy. If reporters are making mistakes pull them aside, kindly and politely, and tell them. You need reporters to disseminate your message and they need you as a source of information.

It's important for you to understand that underestimating the extent of a crisis can be costly, just ask British Petroleum (BP) Oil about the underwater leak in the Gulf of Mexico. That was a classic case of underestimating a crisis.

When a crisis hits what happens within the first few hours is crucial. Whatever the media reports sets the tone for the event, so the first impression that the media gets from you is extremely important. It's better to be proactive than reactive, so please plan ahead. Some day you'll get glad that you did.

Of course, this is just a thumbnail sketch of media crisis planning and it barely scratches the surface. There are many, many fine books out there that offer much greater detail about crisis communications planning. And, again, there are also many fine firms out there specializing in this area. If you really feel that your company or organization could use some professional help in this area, then contact one of those companies to see how much it would cost for them to conduct a one or two-day seminar for you and your staff. In the end, it could be money well spent. If you don't have the money for something like that then I hope this chapter has been or will be helpful to you.

Crisis Management Checklist

Assess Your Needs...

- ✓ Did you develop a plan in advance for a crisis?
- ✓ Did you put together a crisis management team that you can call into action quickly?
- ✓ What are your media objectives?
- ✓ Is your spokesperson springing into action?
- ✓ Did you craft key messages?
- ✓ Have you determined the best channels of communications to use during this crisis?
- ✓ Are you sticking with what you know?
- ✓ Are you being honest and open with reporters and avoiding saying "no comment"?

✓ Are you finding ways to try and relax?

✓ Are you being honest with yourself and determining if you need professional communications help?

Each crisis can be considered unique in nature and might require slightly different responses, depending on the situation. However, it is really important that you have some type of plan in place to handle both internal and external communications matters.

The following steps and suggestions are offered as a guide for you in the event that you are facing a crisis that might involve the media. Crisis communications is different from other types of communications efforts. Hopefully, you will never be faced with such a situation. However, as I've mentioned throughout this book, if you are able to hire professional communications help you should do so, especially in the event of a crisis. Crisis communications really is a specialty and some people who concentrate on that for a living are really worth their price. But if you don't have the money to hire specialists then keep reading and hopefully you'll find the next few pages helpful.

The following is a plan that can be put into place immediately by whoever is the designated person with enough authority.

Depending on the size of your operation, you might want to consider creating or appointing some type of group designated with responding to emergencies, some type of Incident Management Team, designed to complement and enhance your media response plan. This team should be comprised of staff members, personnel or dedicated volunteers who can be quickly called together to help you in time of need. Your designated communications spokesperson can work directly with the Incident Management Team to facilitate distribution of information. Without having some kind of team in place, your job of informing the general public will be much more difficult.

In the event of a CRISIS the designated communications person will have to...

- Determine if an official statement should be prepared and released to the press and the general public.
- With the help of assigned team members, prepare the message.
- Talk with all personnel who are assigned to answer the phone directing them to send all media inquiries to the designated communications person, or those assigned to assist that person.
- Look over and discuss the prepared statement prior to distribution when possible because you don't want to exclude important information, or include something unnecessary.
- Coordinate distribution of information through the media, Web site, publications and direct mail.
- Figure out the best way of sending out a statement to all interested parties. (E-mail? Fax? Text message?)
- Designate someone who will coordinate information gathering from outside authorities.

In the event of a CRISIS, on-going response is crucial, so you really should...

- Assign someone to update all interested parties about changes to or additional details of the situation by some of all of the following methods: voice mail, e-mail, faxes, information hotline, press conferences, media contacts, phone contact, assemblies, letters, newsletters/other publications.
- Figure out how often you should send out updates based upon availability of facts and other factors, like availability of those assigned to speak.
- Pick someone to collect and circulate information until things have returned to the way they were before the crisis.

- Select someone to pay attention to the media coverage of the situation. That person will have to contact media outlets and correct any reported misinformation quickly. Sometimes the right information you distributed is reported incorrectly. You don't want wrong information floating around out there.
- When the crisis is over and things are more normal, assess the success of your plan and make changes as necessary.

Handling media relations during a crisis...

- Frequently the only information your "interested parties" will receive during a crisis is through the media; so, media relations is an important element during crisis communications. Your organization must always be honest and courteous when dealing with the media. If you are not being honest at some point in the distribution of information it will come back to haunt you in some way.
- The designated spokesperson will have to work closely with your designated Incident Management Team in gathering information for interviews, or for the release of general information that is related to their specific areas. Be careful with what information you decide to distribute. Really think hard about what is pertinent and what is not.
- If your staff members or employees are contacted directly by the media, they must without delay inform the designated spokesperson who will handle the media call. Press calls must be funneled to a select group within the organization so that you can make sure that the right information is consistently being released to the public.

Who are your "interested parties"?

There are two types of interested parties that you will be dealing with during a crisis situation. They are the "internal" and "external" interested parties and they are broken down into sub-groups. Depending on your situation, your interested parties might be made up of more than the sub-groups mentioned below.

Internal
- Employees
- Visitors
- Volunteers

External

- Media—Print and Electronic
- Families of Employees
- Families of Visitors
- Board Members (if you have them)
- Local Community-At-Large

Again, depending on your individual situation, you may have more groups to add to these lists. Please list them so that you know who you might have to contact in the event that you are involved in a crisis. You don't want to leave anyone out! It's really a good idea to have these kids of lists written down ahead of time. If things start getting really busy you might end up unintentionally leaving someone out of the loop.

While communicating with the media during a crisis, the designated spokesperson must ...

- Demonstrate that the entire organization is concerned about the people involved.
- Explain what is being done to fix the situation. Explain in detail the steps that you are taking. Make a list. Remember: lists can be your friend.

- Keep the message consistent with all interested parties. Never tell one group anything that is not being told to the media.
- Be open, honest, and tell the full story, to the extent that it is possible. If you do not, someone else will. That's not a risk you want to take. Not being open and honest increases the odds that the crisis team could lose control of the situation.
- Never respond with "no comment." (Have you read that somewhere else in this book?) Instead explain why you cannot answer the question. For example, you do not have those all of the details confirmed at this time, or you will provide the media with an update when you do have an answer to a particular question. Start out by saying something like "We cannot comment at this time because..." And then offer several reasons for your actions.
- Don't guess about anything. If you don't know the answer, just say so and tell those questioning you that you will find the answer and get back to them if possible. Just make sure that you keep this promise.
- Respect reporter deadlines. If you promise to get information, do so as quickly as possible. Respecting their deadlines will reduce the chances that reporters will be badgering you just when you need that the least.
- Never speak off the record. (This probably sounds familiar too, huh?) The media can use any information released. Even if you feel you can speak in confidence to a reporter you might still find that information being reported.
- Never give exclusive interviews during a crisis. All members of the media should have the chance for gathering information. You have to play fair and not play favorites. Playing favorites will come back to haunt you!
- If an injury or death has occurred, do not release the name(s) of the injured/deceased until all next of kin (immediate family) have been notified. The last thing a

family member wants to do is learn about a horrible incident involving a loved one while watching the evening news. Place yourselves in their shoes.

- Do not discuss who is "responsible for the incident", or who is "legally liable" in any way. These types of things have the potential of getting you in more trouble.
- Do not discuss illegal activity. Refer all questions to the appropriate law enforcement agency. It is okay to say things like "Police are investigating. We are cooperating." That's the safest approach.
- Be available at all times. Provide reporters with a pager or cell phone number where they can contact you. You must be accessible to them during a crisis. You want the information going to the press to come from you as the "source."
- Notify receptionists and other employees to direct all media inquiries to the designated spokesperson without speculating on the situation to whoever is calling. A reporter is just doing his/her job and might ask questions of anyone who answers the phone. Besides, the people taking the initial calls are not the spokespeople and they likely don't have all the facts.
- In cases when the media request interviews with family members, offer to provide someone who can act as a liaison to family members for the media so that the family can protect their privacy if that's what they want. However, make sure the media realizes that this person should not be considered the "family spokesperson" unless that's what the family wants.
- Avoid "side comments" meant to be humorous. A crisis isn't the time to entertain. Comments can often be taken out of context. In many cases they are taken out of context or misunderstood.
- Do NOT respond to hypothetical questions. These types of things also can be taken out of context and stretched beyond belief.
- Use everyday language, not jargon that is specific to your line of work, when talking to reporters. Make the

situation as easy to understand as possible. Using job slang or acronyms may not only confuse listeners but they slow things down and are distracting. People at home watching TV or listening to the radio will say to themselves "What did he say?" and they will miss out on important information.

- Provide written materials that give reporters background information. Keep stacks of program brochures or fact sheets handy in case you need them. If you don't have anything like that available it's okay to print information from your Website. In most cases, if the media is responding to a fast-breaking crisis there was no time to print information off the Internet before they left the office.

Immediate response duties checklist…

If you have a designated Incident Management Team, that group will oversee the completion of the steps listed below. If you don't have such a team, I strongly urge you to establish one. During a crisis, various tasks will be assigned by your organization's president, CEO, or designated spokesperson depending on the situation needing attention. An Incident Management Team will prove to be invaluable to you.

It is likely that in the event of a crisis, employees will be recruited to help with implementing the crisis communications plan and other related duties. During emergencies, people from your various departments may be assigned to assist the designated spokesperson and Incident Management Team.

Here are some steps to check:

Step One—First Alert

- o Notify supervisors and designated spokesperson.
- o Ask the switchboard to send all media calls to designated spokesperson.

- o Try to evaluate the situation and level of impact.
- o Decide whether to issue a written media statement or to hold a press briefing.
- o Pick a location for press briefings, the more accessible the better.
- o Notify the media to the time and location of press briefing. Also let the switchboard know in case the press asks about the briefing.

Step Two—Gathering the Facts

- o Put together a list of facts. No rumors.
- o Check with the proper authorities to confirm what's going on.
- o Determine if there are injuries and/or fatalities but do not release the names. Leave that up to the proper authorities.
- o Evaluate the potential for public health risk, if the possibility exists.
- o Determine what authorities (police, fire, etc.) you must and should consult.
- o Talk with responding agencies to coordinate the release of the information you are giving out to the press and the public.
- o Start working on the message that you will release to media and the general public. Make sure that you use the key messages worksheet that you have already created because you've been following all the suggestions in this book.
- o Begin notifying internal, stakeholder audiences from the list that you've already created. You want people in the "inside" learning the facts before they are released to those on the "outside."

Step Three—Verify and Keep the Information Moving

- o Keep written records of the exact times that specific information arrives. You need to record what information is the most recent to make sure that old information does not get released to the press.

o Make sure your facts are straight before you release them. Check with the assisting agencies and with teammates you are working with to make sure that you are all on the same page.

o Keep all of the appropriate interested parties updated on what's going on and do that on a fairly regular basis. "Fairly regular" is something you can determine later.

o Stay in touch with the appropriate government and legal authorities so that they know exactly what's happening.

Step Four—Prepare for Media (Calls and Visits)

o Create a "media contact record" so that you know who has contacted you and when. Sometimes the same media outlets will assign more than one reporter to a story. Keeping a contact record will allow you to say "I've already given that information to someone from your organization. Please check with them."

o Put your designated media spokesperson through a brief rehearsal. Go through "What information media will want" list and rehearse what verified information you plan on making available to the press and the public.

o Discuss how you're going to alert the media. Will it be through press conferences? Written releases? Faxes? All of the above?

o Start getting your pre-arranged media room/ work area ready. This room will be either on or off site. If necessary, establish a work space for reporters to gather the information you'll give them.

o Make sure that before you release any information that you get the approval for your media statement, handout or press release from your president, CEO or manager.

o Pick those officials or team members who will read statements or speak during press conferences or with reporters during interviews.

o   Make sure that everyone within your organization understands your group's guidelines for dealing with the media. You all have to work as a team. You can't afford to have people "striking out on their own."

Step Five — Get Ready for Reporters to Arrive

o   Don't be afraid to ask those folks who say that they are members of the media for identification and ask them to sign in. ALL reporters should carry some kind of press badge or other form of identification. They should be able to provide something more than a business card.

o   Inform the reporters of the restrictions on movement, photography, and videotaping.

o   Stay calm, take a few breaths and start your press briefing.

o   Make sure that you advise media of time and place of next and future updates. It will cut down on the number of calls you'll receive requesting information. Reporters will also like the fact that you are thinking ahead.

o   Remember to follow-up on additional media inquiries and keep any promises that you've made with reporters to "get back to them" if you've been asked a question that you don't have the answer to at the time. However, in those follow-up calls don't reveal new information that you wouldn't give out to everyone else.

Step Six — Media Follow-up & On-going Relations

o   Watch, listen to and read the media coverage to make sure that what's being reported about what's going on is accurate.

o   Ask media outlets for corrections of factual errors, if necessary. You have to set the record straight immediately if reporting mistakes have been made. Just make sure that you are asking in a firm, yet polite manner. Remember that during crises that reporters are under stress too.

- Inform the media of any significant new developments as they happen. You want to be in charge of distributing the information. Basically, you want to tell them about any changes. You don't want them telling you.
- Keep a record of all media contact so that you know which media outlets you are dealing with. This will also help you in your efforts to follow-up and monitor what's being reported.
- Assess the effectiveness of your crisis communications plan and make the appropriate changes as you see fit.

Key Messages List...

Write down the three **Key Messages** that need to be communicated during this crisis. These will be like message points that will serve as the foundation for what you are relaying to your interested parties, both internal and external.

1._____

2._____

3._____

What the media wants to know during crisis situations....

During a breaking news or crisis situation, you will be hit with a lot of questions from reporters. Some of these questions will seem to be very intrusive, or even insensitive. In your wildest dreams you will have never anticipated what some of those questions might be. Below is a list of possible things you could be asked by reporters, as well as your internal and external interested parties.

Remember: information about PEOPLE should always come first. Information about property should follow. Use this list as a guide to prepare your answers needed during a crisis situation:

Casualties

- Number killed or injured or who escaped (use caution with initial numbers and remember to emphasize the numbers are subject to change as the situation evolves).
- Nature of injuries.
- Care given to the people who have been injured.
- The celebrity of anyone, who may have been killed, injured or escaped.

Property Damage

- Estimated value of loss. (Be very careful with estimate numbers because they often change rapidly!)
- Description of property.
- Importance of the property.
- Other property threatened.
- Insurance protection. (Reporters will always ask: Were you insured?)

Causes

- Statements from participants.
- Statements from witnesses.
- Statements from key responders, such as members of your crisis management team, local police and fire department.

How emergency was discovered

- Who was the first to make the report and to whom did they report?
- Who sounded the alarm and alerted the authorities?
- Who called for help, and how quickly that was done?

Rescue and Relief

- The number of people involved in the rescue and relief efforts.
- The names of any prominent people or groups helping.
- The type of rescue equipment being used.
- Any physically disabled persons needing to be rescued.
- How the emergency was prevented from spreading.
- How property was saved.
- Any people you want to thank for pitching in and helping with relief efforts.

Details of the emergency

- Description of the crisis.
- Attempts at escape or rescue.
- Length of time it might take before emergency is over.
- Loss of structures and/or other property.

Incidentals

- Number of spectators, how spectators reacted and crowd control.
- Unusual happenings involved with the emergency.
- State of mind, concerns, or stress of families and survivors. (Be careful: you can't really "speak for someone else" unless you have been designated to do so.)

Legal actions

- Inquests, coroner's reports.
- Police follow-up.
- Insurance company actions.
- Professional negligence or inaction.
- Suits stemming from the incident.

Caution: be extremely careful when handling questions involving legal actions. It's best to NOT address them, if possible. Many times reporters are looking ahead "beyond the crisis" and trying to determine if anyone will be seeking damages. It's really important to steer clear of this. If you are ever asked a question, during a crisis about whether you plan on suing the best response is something like this: "We don't believe that this is the time of place to discuss something like that."

Crisis Meeting Agenda...

During your initial internal briefing about the crisis, you will need to gather some very specific information. You will also have to delegate certain jobs in order to help things run as smoothly as possible.

The following specific agenda items that you should review:

Situation report:

- What happened and what appears to be the cause?
- Gather confirmed facts, such as establishing a chronology of events, determining the consequences, or possible consequences, as you know them.
- Figure out scale of the proposed situation. In other words, how bad things are at the moment.

Initial response status:

- What is being done?
- Who is doing what, and why?
- What are you doing and is it enough?
- When will you begin responding and how long will it take?

Initial communications status:

- Who knows what's going on, who needs to know immediately and later on.

- Let the switchboard know that you will start getting phone calls and have them direct the calls to the right people.

Short-term response requirements:

- Farm out crisis communications responsibilities to team members.
- Figure out what must be done immediately and in the next several hours.
- Figure out what human and material resources are available or needed.

Short-term communication process:

- Staff, faculty, students, families, etc.

Next meeting time.

- Set up your next meeting time and establish information deadlines. Make it clear to your team members that if you've asked them to gather specific information that you need that information by your next meeting. Think of it this way: reporters have deadlines and so do you.

Thing 24

Social Media is a MUST

Pay Attention to Social Media, Bloggers, Online Community Publications

The numbers are pretty overwhelming when it comes to social networking. As I am writing these words, Facebook reports the social networking site has around 700 million members. Amazing! If you don't know about Facebook, or any of the legions of social networking sites, you are either living in a cave, don't own a computer, or you don't have teenage children. If you run a small company, a nonprofit group, or some kind of community organization read further about how social networking can help you.

Social networking has revolutionized communication by allowing people throughout the world to connect in an interactive, digital world. The social networking phenomenon has exploded over the past several years thanks to the proliferation of online communities where users keep in contact with family, friends, colleagues and former classmates.

All of the generations joining Facebook are doing more than socializing. They are using the channel to receive and transmit information, just as previous generations used the newspaper, radio and television for information gathering. Facebook and similar sites are playing larger roles in how people learn about world events. For example, to work around the ban on professional journalists in Iran, supporters of the Iranian opposition candidate used Facebook, Twitter and other social networking sites to inform the world of the violence their government was using to silence them. To increase exposure, some news organizations are making links to their articles available through Facebook and other sites, so that users can share them. You need to join in on the sharing and the socializing.

You have probably been putting it off for a long time, but if you have not jumped into social media with both feet you are missing out on some great (and free!) opportunities to connect with your communities. Even if you are not ready to jump in with both feet, you should at least consider dipping in your big toe. I think you will find that you will see results fairly quickly.

You probably have heard of the Nielson Company. They're mostly known for measuring television viewership, or ratings. But the company does tons of media research, and its research regarding social media is interesting.

- Two-thirds of the developed-world's Internet population visits a social network site of some type.
- Social networks are now the world's fourth most popular online sector after search, portals and software applications.
- Time spent on social network and blogging sites is growing at over three times the rate of overall Internet-usage growth.
- In most countries the percentage of Internet time spent on social networks has doubled.
- Facebook's greatest global growth is in the 35-49 age groups, and the site also has seen growth in the 50-64 age groups.

(Source: Nielsen)

Still not convinced that you need get more social when it comes to social media? In 2010, Ventureneer and Caliber surveyed a bunch of nonprofit organizations to gather information to develop a guide for using social media for marketing and public relations. I suggest that you get a copy of this report and read it. It is called "Nonprofits and Social Media: It Ain't Optional." Read it. It is worth your time.

Basically, the survey and analysis offer great suggestions. Here are a few: Organizations need to develop a solid social media plan and not think that setting up a random Facebook page or Twitter account is enough. Also, if you don't spend the right amount of time in social media, you won't get much out of it. Finally, take the time to learn how to properly use these tools. Don't rush in without a plan or at least some working knowledge of the tools.

Social media allows people to engage in discussions. It gives your followers a place to comment on the great work you do. What would you not want to have a public place where folks can heap a bunch of praise on your organization?

Just think of the awareness raising opportunities that your organization could take advantage of in the social media environment. If you went online right now (yes, put a bookmark in place right now) and did a random search of nonprofits or community organizations and visited their websites, you would see that many if not most of them invite you to visit them on Facebook, to "friend" them, or click the "like" button. What does this do? This helps spread the word about that organization at no real cost, other than the time it takes to visit.

Many organizations now use social networks to help raise money while they are raising awareness. Just think of the possibilities. If you are looking to add to your membership, if you are looking to recruit or mobilize people, what better way than to do it through a social networking site, that costs you NOTHING to operate?

The social media tools are free, but the time needed to do it right are not. However, if you want to be visible, if you want people to notice and know about your nonprofit, community group or cause, you cannot afford to do social media.

Check out this list of the top 15 Most Popular Social Networking Sites according to eBizMBA:

- Facebook
- Twitter
- LinkedIn
- MySpace
- Ning
- Tagged
- Orkut
- Hi5
- Myyearbook
- Meetup
- Badoo
- Mylife
- Friendster
- Multiply

Google is also dipping its high tech toes in the social networking scene with the establishment of something called Google+ (Plus). At the time of this writing, Google is calling its endeavor a "project." There is no doubt that the list of social networking options will continue growing.

So, if you do decide to start a Facebook page for your organization – and I hope that you do – here are a few things to keep in mind. It is important that when you post information make sure that you posts with a purpose. Make sure that the information you are putting out there is meaningful. Fewer things will erode your credibility than random, silly postings that are meaningless.

Make sure that the content you are creating really matters to the people you really want to reach. If you are someone operating a nonprofit to benefit abandoned pets would it make sense for you to post information about your recent vacation? No, it would not. However, if you were to post announcements about an upcoming fundraiser, or you were inviting folks to a meeting now that would be the proper information to post.

Make sure that you place the right person in charge of your social networking efforts. Maybe your best friend's teenage son knows a lot about the Internet and social networking, but is he the right person for this task? If you operate an organization, it is best that you have one to three people within your group who are considered "site administrators" who have the ability to post official announcements on your social networking page.

Use your Facebook page, or whatever you launch, to help drive traffic to your website (Please tell me you have a website!) And use your website to drive people to your social network page. Having multiple presences in the digital world is an excellent way to reach more potential clients, members, or contributors.

If you really want to learn the ins and outs of social media and really want to use it to its full advantage consider taking classes. Local chambers of commerce often offer workshops. If your local chambers don't have anything, just do a simple Internet search to see what's out there in your community. I guarantee that you will be able to find classes and seminars on how to use social media to make your business grow, or how to raise awareness about your organization.

Remember that the social network page you eventually create (and you ARE going to create one) should reflect your mission and brand. You really need to make sure the content is contains reflects what you want people to see and know about you. You have control over the content, so you that advantage to the fullest.

You can start conversations that are important to you and your cause and you can ask others to join in and comment. You can create a direct connection with the people with whom you want to directly connect. You can empower your followers (i.e. "friends", clients) and ask them to do something. You are not necessarily selling a physical product, but you are selling your organization, in a way.

By allowing followers to post updates, photos, videos and comments on your social network site, you are engaging the public. You are getting your name out there. And you are getting help from other people to do that. And remember, the only thing you are really spending is your time.

And while we are on the subject, please do not forget about YouTube. I am sure that you all have visited YouTube as some time or another. Someone sent you a link to a video of a kitten trying to crawl out of a cookie jar, or there's a video of a youth league baseball coach who gets accidentally smacked between the legs by one of his players who is swinging a bat. But you also can use YouTube to post short videos about your organization. You can even create your own YouTube channel. You can post links to those videos on your Facebook page as a way of telling more people about what your group or organization does. It does not cost you anything to do this either, except for the investment of time.

Keep in mind that jumping into the social media mix is not without problems. While these virtual communities allow people to easily connect with others; those connections are not always positive. Social networks frequently leave members vulnerable to privacy invasion, identity theft, copyright infringement and a host of other legal threats and ethical challenges. These are concerns not characteristically connected with conventional media usage. So when you proceed, please proceed with some caution. Maybe not caution, but awareness.

However, nonprofits, small businesses and community groups should be the leaders in social media. If you are involved with one of these types of groups, you will find that social media is the best way to engage with the stakeholders that you want and need to reach.

I really strongly dislike the term "thinking outside the box", but I want to encourage you do so as you begin making your many media connections. When you begin putting together your list of media agencies to target with your information, I really want you to go beyond the traditional outlets of newspaper, television and radio. Why? There's a lot more media out there and it's growing every single day.

When you are trying to connect with the media please don't forget to contact the UNCONVENTIONAL as well as the conventional media. What do I mean by unconventional? I don't mean tabloid newspapers under investigation for hacking into people's voicemail, or TV talking heads that unabashedly lean to the left or right politically while they masquerade as journalists. I am talking about bloggers, community news websites and message boards. These are the types of outlets where more people are getting their news and information and these are the types of media folks you should contact to help others learn more about your organization or small company.

You would be surprised to find the number of online publications operating on the Internet that are just like those small community newspapers that operate and publish news stories about what's going on in YOUR community. These are online publications that are often hungry, no starving, for content. And you are just the right person to provide that content. Sure, these publications are not on the level of the online version of the New York Times or the Los Angeles times, but they are visited every single day by the same people that you want to have visiting your store, joining your organization, or partnering with or even contributing to your nonprofit.

It is important to remember that these small online publications will not come looking for you. You have to come looking for them. You have to take the time and make the time to build relationships with the people who publish these online community publications. I promise that you will not regret making these connections. It will pay off.

You also need to spend some time surfing the Internet for blogs. Do your homework. It will take you some time investment in the way of research, but do everything you can to get the name and contact information for bloggers, community news websites, and message boards that might be visited by the same people that you want to connect with. Build a list of the blogs you wish to contact. Find the name of the editor, and if the blog has other contributors, found out those names too. See if there is a contact email address listed on the blog. See if there is a contact form that you can fill out and use to send messages. You should start sending messages and making contact with these people. Introduce yourself and your cause. Tell the writer/editor/blogger why you are making contact.

When you make your pitch please make sure that the blogger you are trying to connect with blogs about the type of information you are pitching him or her. It's like making a bad sales pitch. In your message, don't forget to include your website address or your fan page on Facebook, if you have one.

Do people really read blogs? Yeah, they do. According to a report from Comscore, partly sponsored by Gawker Media and SixApart, 30 percent of all Internet users in the United States are regular blog visitors. According to that report, blog readers are online an average of 23 hours online per week, whereas the average Internet user is online roughly 13 hours per week. Either way, that's a lot of people spending a lot of time online who could be learning a lot more about you and your organization if you could connect with bloggers.

A Few Words about YouTube

Depending on which research you read, some estimates say close to 100 million people are on YouTube every day. While that's a lot of people looking at videos of cats playing the piano, or budding pop stars performing to sellout crowds at community social halls, it is also a lot of people who could be learning about your organization or small company. You never know what videos can become popular, and why can't one of those videos be one that you've created?

Producing a brief video or series of videos about your group and posting them on YouTube can be a very, very easy thing to do. All you need is a digital video camera and some sort of video editing program. You don't need the most expensive camera or the most elaborate video editing system, unless you have the money to spend. Start slow and simple. Post these videos on YouTube and send the links to friends and ask them to send those links to their friends. You also can post these links directly on your Facebook, or website. Send messages to anyone and everyone you can think of asking them to check out your video. Doing so increases the chances of someone else seeing these videos and learning more about you or your organization. You also can create your own YouTube channel where you can continue posting videos. It is definitely worth the time and effort it would take.

Thing 25

YOU can communicate WITHOUT the media

Other ways to communicate in your community

It is really important for you to have a presence in your local community if you want to be successful with getting your name in the media. Outreach is a crucial element for success. People need to know who you are and that is possible if they are used to seeing your name all over the place. How can that be done?

Before you read any further please realize that I am making these suggestions for a couple of reasons: they go a long way to contributing to the image of your business or group, but also remember that community service is good for the soul. It never hurts to give something back.

Here are some simple and inexpensive ways for you to be a part of your community, gain visibility and get your group's name out there:

- Join or have executive level members of your organization join local task forces, boards, commissions, civic committees or any kind of group that caters to the local community. Such groups include but are not limited to: scholarship committees, food banks, family shelters, committees dedicated to cleaning up communities, and youth sports organizations. By getting more involved you are helping people gain a better understanding of who you are and what you do and, in turn, learn more about your organization. It is a quiet and subtle way of getting your name out in the public.
- If you operate a small or medium sized company consider "adopt" a nonprofit organization as a fund

raising pet project in which you help that organization raise money, stage events or attract new members. Not only will you and your employees and staff members get a good feeling of satisfaction from such a project, but feature stories in local newspapers often include rosters of folks who are "pitching in to make a difference." You could be among those being recognized.

- If you have a large enough meeting room at your site consider making it available at no cost to small, outside organizations, civic groups and church organizations that might be in need of an occasional meeting place. Seniors groups, parent organizations and other social service clubs are often looking for meeting space.

- Make sure that your organization, group or company has a presence in community events. Organize teams for walk-a-thons and other goodwill fund raisers. Set up booths where you can distribute information. Not only is this good "face time" out in the community, it also helps build camaraderie and a team spirit within your organization.

- Place entries in local parades. Build floats or place placards on cars and participate in processions down Main Street. People will see your group's name and remember who you are. You will be known as being kind hearted members of the local community – which you probably are any way.

- If there's a local carnival or festival in your community ask if you can place a booth there somewhere on the grounds where you and other staff members can distribute material about your group or company. Make sure you have large colorful signs on display so that you'll get noticed. There's usually a slight fee for getting booth space but it's a small investment with a potentially larger payoff.

- Sponsor Little League teams. Parents are sitting around in a park on a Saturday morning watching teams sponsored by local businesses running around and having fun, which goes a long way toward spreading goodwill. Team sponsorships can be fairly inexpensive.

- Accept a volunteer position that's high visibility. If you are the local chairman or president for a special fund drive, or the lead organizer for a major benefit event media exposure can often come along with it.
- If there are some area businesses that you often partner with on projects ask if they would be willing to have some of your program information (brochures, pamphlets, posters) on display in their lobby or main meeting room. You can offer to return the favor for them. And if you are going to do that consider creating a lobby display with a heading that reads something like "Our Community Partners" or something along those lines. This shows great community involvement.

Again, I know that much of what I've mentioned in this segment sounds calculating and self-serving. In some respects, you could make that argument. You are well aware that becoming more visible through community service type of involvement can spill over into opportunistic press coverage. But the flip side is that you will get more out of community involvement than just a good reputation. You'll gain real satisfaction as well.

Now, time to get off my soapbox.

Thing 26

Media Relations and Public Relations and Marketing are All DIFFERENT Things

What's the difference between media relations and marketing? And what about PR?

Many people confuse the terms "media relations", "marketing" and "public relations" and use those terms interchangeably. It's easy to understand why people are confused with these terms and their meanings because their paths typically cross.

There are similarities among them. However, keep in mind that there are subtle differences and because there are differences you want make sure you know what they are. You might ask, why? Well, you don't want to hire a media relations specialist when what you really need is marketing help or assistance with public relations. You don't want to sign a contract with a marketing firm when what you really need is help with media relations. Some forms do it all. However, you don't want to contract with anyone and spend big money unnecessarily if this is something that you can, and should, do yourself.

What is "communications or media relations"?
Media relations and/or communications involve those activities dealing directly with the people in charge of making editorial decisions at media outlets such as television and radio stations, newspapers. This can also involve the decision makers who are working with magazines, online magazines and association newsletters.

People working in media relations should understand how newsrooms work and who to contact to create interest in possible news items. They should be skilled in writing press releases, media advisories, Web site content and speeches. They should know when it's appropriate to contact an editor, a reporter or a columnist and how to contact them.

Communications experts are the folks – in most cases former journalists or people with journalism training - who handle inquiries from reporters and know how to respond in a timely fashion. They should know how to provide reporters with information, connect those reporters with knowledgeable sources, and speak in a language that reporters understand. By that I mean, in short declarative sentences and sound bites, using no confusing jargon.

Communications experts should understand exactly what a reporter means when he or she asks for something and explains the constraints involved in their quest for information. This person needs to understand deadlines and what elements the reporter needs, and doesn't need.

In other words, they work almost like journalists, only they are working for those being contacted by the media.

Media relations professionals must also know how to work to get the name of their company, group or organization in the news. It should be their goal to "shop around" stories of potential interest to reporters and writers to get them interested in covering them, or their issues. (This is why people often confuse media relations with public relations.)

Also, communications professionals deal with all forms of communications within the organization, such as what content is provided in fact sheets, brochures and fliers. This should also include Web site content, internal messages to staff through newsletters and memos.

What is "public relations"?
There are some similarities between media relations and public relations (PR), but there are also some differences. Public relations folks are interested in many of the same things as the communications specialists. However, the functions of a public relations professional also include ongoing activities to make

sure the company, group or organization has a strong public image. Media relations folks are concerned about image too, but it's really a specialty and a focus for PR folks.

One of the major differences between a communications person and a PR person is that public relations activities also include helping the public to understand the company and its products. Public relations and sales divisions of major companies (should) work closely together for the good of the company. Public relations experts frequently conduct business through the media, by getting stories placed in newspapers and magazines and on radio and television stations. PR is often considered a primary activity that is included in promotion.

Publicity is successful when your company, organization or group is mentioned – hopefully favorably - in the media. As is mentioned in another section of this book, organizations don't have control over the message put out by the media, but ONLY the message they give to the media. When it comes right down to it, reporters, editors and writers decide what will be reported and what will not. Please remember that this is something you cannot control.

To add more information to this mix… public relations often also involves advertising. Unless you live in a cave, don't read the papers, don't own a radio or TV and never read anything you know that advertising is bringing a product or service to the attention of the public. In your case the public means potential and current customers, potential or current members, or constituents. Advertising is done in a number of ways through the print and electronic media and involve person-to-person contact, pre-produced commercials, billboards, signs, brochures, direct mailings or e-mail messages.

What is "marketing"?
If you want the official definition of marketing then turn to the experts. According to the American Marketing Association, marketing is "an organizational function and a set of processes

for creating, communicating and delivering value to customers and for managing customer relationships in ways that benefit the organization and its stakeholders".

That's a little long-winded but what does that mean exactly? Let's turn to a different definition. The Dictionary of Marketing Terms calls marketing a "process of planning and executing the conception, pricing, promotion, and distribution of ideas, goods, and services to create exchanges that satisfy individual and organizational goals."

Still not sure?

Well, basically marketing included several wide ranging and closely linked activities. The main goal of marketing is to make sure you are meeting your customer's needs and getting something in return. When marketing is done well it involves a lot of research and study. For example, with market research you could focus on seeking answers to the following questions:

- What groups make up our potential clients?
- What are the needs of our potential clients?
- What needs are we capable of meeting?
- How can we meet these needs?
- What techniques should be used to attract and persuade customers?

Bear in mind that marketing focuses on products, but that the products we are talking about are not only "products" in the literal sense, but also things like the services your organization or group can provide. Products can also mean the special classes you offer, if you are a school district. It could also mean the cause you represent, if you are a social service organization.

Marketing also goes in depth and includes analysis of the competition, where your new products fit in the market, how much you should charge, and also promoting those products through advertising, promotions, and public relations.

Can you see how all of these areas of communications tend to intertwine? There are similarities and differences at the same time.

The goal of marketers is to recruit and keep new customers. The goal of public relations is to spread the word to new customers. The goal of communications is to tell people – inside and outside the organization – about the new products the company has that with which they are trying to attract customers.

So as you begin figuring out your communications needs put a lot of thought into determining what you really need; communications, public relations, marketing or all of the above. Also try and decide whether you have the budget to hire a professional, or professionals, to perform those duties for you. If you don't have the money please realize that there are ways for you to learn to do some of those things for yourself, but at the same time recognize that whatever communications related job you take on will be an investment in time and effort.

Thing 27
Know What They Are Saying about YOU

Monitoring the media

Watching and reading what they say about you...
Finally, when all is said and done you need to evaluate your news coverage. It's simple to do and it's important. You want to make sure that your outreach efforts have paid off.

- Read the newspapers. Listen to the radio. Watch the TV news. See what they've done with the information you've given them.
- Collect your news clippings and analyze them. See how you were quoted. See if your planning paid off. Keep a file of your press clippings to document coverage. If possible, keep files of video clips from television news reports as well as audio clips from radio stations. Use them to build a portfolio which you can use for marketing efforts. Also consider using these clips on your organization's website as a way of letting the viewing public know that you have been "in the news."
- Make sure that people in positions of influence within your organization and outside of it are aware of the coverage you've received or are receiving. This will let them know that your media relations plan, the one that you've started building after reading this book, is starting to pay off handsomely.
- Don't forget that it is appropriate to follow up with the press by way of phone calls and thank you notes. If you didn't like the tone of the story, tell the reporter. Do so in a polite way, of course. If you were misquoted, say so. Ask for a correction if the errors are glaring.
- If you really like the story the reporter did then let that reporter know. A hand written note or even a quick e-mail will work wonders. It will let the reporter know he or she did a good job. And it might lead to future,

positive coverage.

Gauging your success

Measuring the effectiveness of your media plan
Sometimes it's not easy to quantify the effectiveness of your communications plan. First, you have to figure out for yourself exactly what "success" means to you. You must be realistic from the beginning. It's good to set the bar high, but not too high.

Here are some simple ways to gauge the success of your efforts to reach out to the media:

- The number of people attending an event
- The number of phone calls and letters you've received after coverage
- The number of calls received from people interested in volunteering for your group or program
- The increase in financial contributions - if you are a nonprofit- or the increase in clients if you are a business.

If you really want to get technical and scientific, you can get an idea of how many people actually saw that story about you on the local television news or heard it on the radio. TV and radio stations are constantly monitored to let broadcast executives know how many people are tuning in. It's possible for the electronic news folks to tell you "approximately" how many people saw or heard a story at any given time.

You can also estimate the number of people who read about you in the newspaper because print publications measure readership in terms of "circulation". However, keep in mind that circulation numbers will tell you how many people bought a newspaper but not necessarily how many people read about you and your organization or group in that newspaper.

Be careful how you brag about these numbers—if you choose to—because they are estimates for the most part.

Thing 28

Remember That YOU Get Out of It What YOU Put Into It

Basic Steps in Building Communications/PR Program

- Research
- Analysis & Planning
- Implementation
- Planning
- Evaluation

If you are really determined to develop a communications/public relations plan that will be the envy of the world then keep reading this chapter. However, if you don't want to get too involved in constructing a big media master plan, then go ahead and skip this chapter and move onto the next one. (Although, you might want to read this one any way.)

If you want effective communications and public relations programs, there are five basic steps that need to be followed. Actually, there are probably more than five but we are just going over the essentials here.

First, you need to do your **research** to find out what your audiences think about you and what information they need. Depending on your profession, those audiences can be anyone: customers, clients, members, young people, old people, shepherds or whatever. For nonprofit groups, the audience is the general public, the people you are trying to reach. For schools, the audience consists of parents, students and people living in your community.

In conducting your research, you have to spend some time meeting these folks in your audience and talking with them. Conduct surveys, either formal or informal. If you want to really get serious – and have the money to do it – there are all kinds of private companies that can dive into the research for you. The results likely will be worth it in the long run, but be ready to put out some good money for it. If you are doing this on your own invest some time to analyze what you found out in talking to those members of your audience and plan how to meet their needs.

After you've spent some time with these folks, determining their wants and needs, sit down and start **planning** your course of action. Start asking yourself these types of questions:

- Who is it that we are trying to reach, and what do they want?
- How can we reach these people?
- What kind of budget are we working with: small, medium, large, non-existent?
- In an effort to get our story out to the public should we stage press conferences, community forums, make contacts with local newspaper editors?
- Is there anyone working within our group that can help with the workload or am I going to be doing all of this myself?
- Are we just looking for instant media gratification, or is this a long term plan?
- Are there any alliances we can form with other groups like ours because there is strength in numbers?

You could probably come up with countless questions. Just keep asking yourself questions until you feel you've explored every option possible.

After the **analysis and planning** is complete, you have to communicate what has been learned. That communication is both internal – to employees and staff – and external – to the audiences. It's really important that you let staff members, or at least the high level staff members (if you have them), know what you are doing and how you are trying to enhance the visibility of your company, group or organization. This will help them feel more involved with the operation, and they might even have some good input. Remember: no one has ever cornered the market on good ideas!

That brings us to the **implementation** of your plan. If you have covered all the steps we've talked about over the past few pages then the actual implementation will hopefully be the easiest and smoothest part of the process. As you read further through this book you will pick up more tools to help you through this process.

Implementation could take a short period of time, or a long period of time. It really depends on what your objectives are. Do you just want the press to cover your big community forum, or are you really trying to establish a long-term relationship with the press so that you might be called upon periodically for interviews? Put some thought into your objectives before you act.

The final step involves the **evaluation** of the results. Did your plan work? Was it effective? Did you reach the people you were trying to reach? There are plenty of ways to determine the effectiveness of your efforts. That will be explained in more detail later.

Keep in mind that the evaluation process can help you determine if you are following the right path. That way you can use the same plan for your next effort.

Read on and find out more.

Planning Questions...

Think Hard as You Answer These Questions

- Who is it that we are trying to reach, and what do they want?

- How can we reach these people?
- What kind of budget are we working with: small, medium, large, non-existent?
- In an effort to get our story out to the public should we stage press conferences, community forums, make contacts with local newspaper editors?
- Is there anyone working within our group that can help with the workload or am I going to be doing all of this myself?
- Are we just looking for instant media gratification, or is this a long term plan?
- Are there any alliances we can form with other groups like ours because there is strength in numbers?

Thing 29

Figure Out If You Can Do This YOURSELF

Should you hire a full-time communications specialist? The answer: that depends...

Many companies, organizations and groups wrestle with the question of whether to have a full-time communications specialist on staff. There are many pros and cons to consider when making this decision.

Let's go over the cons first, not because I am a negative person but because I want to get them out of the way, and because I am MORE in favor of companies having full-time media people than not. That is, of course, if hiring a communications person is a financial option for you or your organization.

Having someone on staff dedicated solely to doing media related work is worth considering, however:

- Do you have room in the budget to make the kind of financial commitment necessary when hiring a full-time media professional? The position would cost a small company, or any company for that matter, a good chunk of money. Make sure there's enough money in your bucket before taking the leap.
- Are you really going to be doing enough media outreach project possibilities to justify having a communications director or some other kind of media specialist working for you all the time? If there are not enough projects being planned or produced then you are under-employing someone and over-extending your spending.
- What kind of impact will it have on your tiny, multi-tasking staff if you have one person doing only one job? Many small – and even medium sized organizations – employ people who wear many hats and perform many

duties. You might have a hard time justifying the position to other staff members – and even yourself – especially if the media person does not produce stellar results, if any results at all.

- Ask yourself if you are only hiring a full-time media person in order to brag about it at the local chamber of commerce brown bag luncheons every Tuesday afternoon? If you are trying to give the illusion to your business friends and competitors that you can "play ball with the big boys" then you had better think long and hard about your decision. If this is your justification then you are making a mistake.

Many medium sized businesses and organizations have full-time media relations or public relations people on staff, and they work very hard because they are usually a one-person operation. Small companies rarely have an employee solely dedicated to media. It's usually not something that fits into the budget. You have to decide for yourself what's right for you and your organization.

Now, let's look at the pro side of the pro/con list regarding the debate over keeping a full-time communications person on staff. Here are some good reasons why it's worth considering:

- A full-time communications professional can contribute to the development of your organization's overall strategic plan, especially if that plan includes a facet of media relations – and hopefully it does.
- If you have a strategic plan – and let's hope you do – the communications professional can help support you in enacting your plan and assist in explaining the plan to employees or staff members.
- Since all groups, organizations and companies have specific interests a full-time communications staffer can develop policies, procedures and materials to help you "tell your story".
- You will get a better fix on the "pulse of the local

community" by having a person on the job dedicated to doing just that.

- Having an employee solely focused on getting your group or organization's name "out there" improves those chances. It also saves high level employees from having to worry about media matters while still keeping the place running.
- Having a communications person on staff provides you with someone who can represent the organization out in the community, who can take all calls from the press, and who can concentrate on trying to get media outlets to report news stories about your company, group or organization.

Again, this argument boils down to money. I know it sounds like I am being repetitive, redundant and repetitive. However, if you have the money to keep somebody on full-time to deal with the media, then go ahead and do so.

If you can't justify a full-time hire then consider hiring someone on a part-time contract. There are plenty of good media relations firms out there who will take you on as a project and they will do good work.

Most likely, you probably don't have the budgetary room for a hire like this of any kind, and that's why you bought this book.

It is possible for small and medium sized companies, organizations and nonprofits, to handle media relations fairly well without having a communications director or media relations manager on staff. Just remember that it's an investment in time and effort to do things correctly.

Thing 30

None of These Things Will Do You Any Good Unless EVERYONE within Your Group Is On Board

The Team Approach

Make sure every employee is ON THE TEAM!
Perception is everything. Henry Ford once said: "Coming together is a beginning, staying together is progress, and working together is success."

It is very important to make sure that every employee/staff member is part of your team. That does not mean that every employee will serve as a spokesperson, give interviews, or answer questions from the press. It means that everyone within your organization needs to understand the impact of statements made about the organization and how the public perceives what is being said.

This goes for everything from casual conversations by employees who are within earshot of members of the general public - and possibly even the media - to the way employees and staff members speak with people, whether they are meeting at conferences or in the front lobby of the building.

Everyone within your organization or group, every employee, has to realize the great impact of what he or she says or does. Every statement heard by someone in the general public helps form an impression about your group and what it does. Everyone within your organization must think of himself or herself as a member of the team sharing the same important, positive message.

All winning teams are goal-oriented. Make improved communications your goal.

Final Communications Checklist

Yet another checklist to help you formulate your plan!

1. Does your office have a policy outlining your communication goals and objectives?
   ( ) Yes ( ) No ( ) Let me get back to you on that!

2. Does this policy have a detailed, step-by-step implementation plan?
   ( ) Yes ( ) No ( ) Let me get back to you on that!

3. Does your plan emphasize planning and coordination involving every member of your team?
   ( ) Yes ( ) No ( ) Let me get back to you on that!

4. Do you have a plan for dealing with all types of crisis and does that plan include the media?
   ( ) Yes ( ) No ( ) Let me get back to you on that!

5. Have you expressed to your staff/employees the importance of good communications throughout your group, company or organization?
   ( ) Yes ( ) No ( ) Let me get back to you on that!

6. Do you believe communications training is important for you and members of your group, company or organization?
   ( ) Yes ( ) No ( ) Let me get back to you on that!

7. Do you use staff meetings as a way to communicate with staff/employees and to receive feedback?
   ( ) Yes ( ) No ( ) Let me get back to you on that!

8. Overall, do you believe that you are you trained and equipped to deal with the media?
   ( ) Yes ( ) No ( ) Let me get back to you on that!

About The Author

Tim Herrera is an author who has done just about everything a person can do in media: college writing and communications instructor, newspaper columnist, television news reporter, radio reporter and anchor, TV news anchor, free-lance writer, talk show host and Communications Director.

Tim spent 22 years in the journalism business, with most of that time spent honing his public speaking skills in television and radio. For 12 years, he was a reporter and anchor at KCRA-TV in Sacramento where he earned the reputation as one of the market's top television journalists and was the winner of 14 prestigious journalism awards. He has also worked as a television and radio reporter and anchor in Dallas-Fort Worth and Pittsburgh. Tim was a runner-up for the 2003 Will Rogers Humanitarian Award, presented by the National Society of Newspaper Columnists. He has a B.A. in Journalism and an M.A. in Strategic Communications.

Tim is the author of hundreds of freelance articles and columns. He has also authored four books: *"Dad, You Are NOT Going Out Wearing That!"*, *"From Wedgies to Feeding Frenzies"*, *"Where the Dust Never Settles"* and *"I'm Their Dad! Not Their Babysitter!"* All four books are collections of warm and amusing essays on family and parenthood.

Tim also has extensive experience in media relations having served as Communications Director for several agencies for the State of California including the Department of Consumer Affairs and the Department of Conservation. He currently serves as the Communications Director for the Sacramento County Office of Education where he has earned numerous awards from the California School Public Relations Association (CalSPRA).

For more information visit his Web site: www.timherrera.com.

Other Books by Tim Herrera

30 Things You Should Know About Media Relations
First Edition

Dad, You Are NOT Going Out Wearing That!
Chronicles of Middle Aged Fatherhood

From Wedgies to Feeding Frenzies:
A Semi Survival Guide for Parents of Teens

Where the Dust Never Settles
Mostly Truthful Tales of Hectic Family Life

I'm Their Dad! Not Their Babysitter!
Essays, Anecdotes and War Stories Celebrating Fatherhood

College Courses and Writing Seminars

Principles of Communication in Healthcare

Introduction to Human Communication

Communication Technologies

Introduction to College Reading & Writing

Elements of University Competition & Communication

Media Relations Made Easy

Basic Dos and Don'ts When Dealing with Media

Words to Live by In Media Relations

Developing a Communications Plan

Writing the Personal Essay

Writing about Your Own Experiences

30 Things You Should Know About Media Relations (First Edition)
was selected as the 2009 Best How-To Non-Fiction book by
Northern California Publishers and Authors.

Book Cover Photo Courtesies

I wanted to offer special thanks to the Sacramento County Office of Education (SCOE) for the use of two of photos on the back cover: the portrait and the photo at the podium.

The classroom photo was taken during a seminar "Writing about Your Own Experiences" taught during the annual Our Life Stories Conference at Consumnes River College in May 2010.

The photo with Air Force One in the background was taken in October of 1993. We would have gotten closer but the nice men wearing dark glasses and dark suits smiled but strongly suggested we keep our distance.